EMPOWERMENT AND ESTATE REGENERATION

A critical review

Murray Stewart and Marilyn Taylor

99

9

J

10

the POLICY

P ~ P

P R E S

First published in Great Britain in 1995 by

The Policy Press
University of Bristol
Rodney Lodge
Grange Road
Bristol BS8 4EA

Telephone: (0117) 973 8797
Fax: (0117) 973 7308
E-mail: tpp@bris.ac.uk

© The Policy Press, 1995

ISBN 1 86134 001 X

Murray Stewart is Professor of Urban Government at the School for Policy Studies, but is shortly to be joining the Faculty of the Built Environment at the University of the West of England. **Marilyn Taylor** is Reader in Social Policy in the Department of Community Studies at the University of Birmingham.

The Policy Press wor⬛⬛⬛⬛⬛⬛⬛⬛⬛⬛⬛⬛f gender, race, disability, age and s⬛⬛⬛⬛⬛⬛⬛⬛

Printed in Great Brit⬛⬛⬛⬛⬛⬛⬛⬛⬛⬛n.

CONTENTS

ACKNOWLEDGEMENTS

Our thanks go to the Joseph Rowntree Foundation, whose support made this study possible, and in particular to John Low, whose encouragement and advice proved essential throughout the project. In addition, we would wish to thank members of the Action for Estates Programme Advisory Group for their comments on an early draft. Within the then School for Advanced Urban Studies, Pete North undertook an extensive bibliographic search, while Jenny Capstick and Angela Templeman offered typing support.

For the final preparations for what is one of the first publications from The Policy Press at Bristol, we are indebted to Dawn Pudney and Julia Mortimer for their efforts in editing, production and marketing, and to Alison Shaw for initial publishing advice.

Finally, we thank each other for the pleasure of working together. While we go our separate ways, our commitment to the principles of collaborative and mutually supportive work remain, hopefully to be resurrected in future work together.

Marilyn Taylor, University of Brighton
Murray Stewart, University of the West of England

SUMMARY

The historical perspective

Over the past 30 years there has been a radical shift in the ideological and political context within which involvement, participation and empowerment have been conducted. A reliance of state provision has given way to a market culture emphasising consumer choice and control. Despite many years of experience and experiment in regeneration, the lessons from the literature of community development and estate regeneration have still to be absorbed.

A framework of analysis

The most marked feature of the past 30 years has been the failure to address basic issues about how power operates, or to acknowledge the ways in which agendas continue to be set by authorities, on the basis of perceptions and assumptions over which people living on estates have little or no control. Although it has now been acknowledged that residents need to be involved in regeneration initiatives, the ways in which existing power relationships in the political and professional arena are continuously reinforced have yet to be addressed.

In principle, power can be achieved at the individual or collective level. Many methods have been tried, and experience suggests that a combination of approaches is most likely to be effective.

Housing

Tenant organisations have a long history and there is considerable literature on the principles and practice of participation. Encouraging greater tenant control over housing requires commitment on all sides, resources and time. Locally delivered services have brought benefits, but the potential of 'exit' to empower people on the margins of the housing market has so far been limited.

Economy and employment

There are few job opportunities on many estates, nor is there any basic right to work.   Opportunities for individuals to empower themselves require increased education, training and access to job opportunities – on many estates there are examples of local economic development agencies offering a cluster of training, job access, placement and job creation support. There are, however, instances where such agencies are at odds with local residents as community needs and priorities conflict with commercial criteria.

Social consumption

The recent emphasis on the physical renewal of housing and on economic regeneration reinforces the long-standing position of social provision as the poor relation of estate-based initiatives. There is a need to acknowledge social concerns more widely – too little has been done to link environmental improvement and physical renewal with local employment creation.

Area-wide initiatives

'Partnership' between the government, the private sector and the community is the watchword of the mid-1990s. The extent to which it offers more power to residents on estates is so far ambiguous. Engagement with partnership demands a great deal of community representatives and poses new challenges for the articulation and representation of community interests – the rules of engagement are still dictated by the more powerful parties.

Conclusions

Estate residents are caught in a spiral of disempowerment:

- poverty – lack of basic rights to income and work

- marginalisation through poor housing, limited job opportunities, poor infrastructure, poor health, inaccessibility, stereotyping and low quality services

- lack of confidence, breakdown in social interaction and mutual support expressed in individual and collective isolation

- lack of influence or control over the way local services are delivered to residents

- lack of involvement in decisions that affect the area.

These levels of disempowerment can be contrasted with parallel structures of empowerment:

- building local capacity and releasing existing strengths

- changing the nature of service delivery

- strengthening the foundations of area decision making and governance

- shifting underlying structures of society.

Sustainability is a key element in the empowerment process – it is central to the question of how to encourage stable, confident and self-governing communities. The energies and resources that may be brought together in partnerships must be tied to a long-term view well beyond the life of individual political administrations – this, above all, is the reason for building real power in estates. Politicians, professionals and external agencies come and go – it is the residents who will go on living on estates and whose children will be born and who will live there.

Conclusion

INTRODUCTION

This report is the outcome of a review commissioned by the Joseph Rowntree Foundation of the literature and experience on empowerment and estate regeneration. The project forms part of the Joseph Rowntree Foundation Action on Estates Programme.

Since the 1960s there has been a steady stream of initiatives within the broad traditions of public participation and community development, aiming in different ways and with different objectives to support the regeneration of local estates or neighbourhoods and the empowerment of communities and their residents. Much of the experience on estate regeneration, however, has been fitful, the effects have often been transitory, the impacts have been disputed and the consistent messages ignored. Estate regeneration has as often been the arena for divisive and weakening conflict between local people and authority (often the local authority) as for the building of resident or community power.

There is little consensus about either the appropriate theoretical basis for regeneration and empowerment or the conclusions that can be drawn from the empirical evidence. International experience offers at best an ambiguous message, not least the experience from the United States, from which many strands of British urban-based community development emerged (Hambleton and Taylor, 1993).

This review provides an overview of the literature and the policy developments of the past 30 years in order to draw out general lessons about the nature of the empowerment process. It is not a good practice guide or a manual to empowerment. The final report (forthcoming) on the whole Action on Estates Programme will offer more immediate guidelines for policy and its implementation.

In carrying out the review we have drawn on a wide range of sources, although we would not claim that they are comprehensive. In general we have relied upon written material, and as far as possible on 'researched' studies of estates, or at the minimum, on considered reflections on estate-based practice. We have also drawn on information about the work that has been supported under the umbrella of the Joseph Rowntree Foundation Action on Estates Programme. In the course of the review we have found some areas where the literature, at least on estate-based empowerment, is relatively silent (for example, education, health, alcohol and substance abuse). We have also found remarkably little reference to the position of women or ethnic minorities on estates.

The report falls into three parts. The first part, chapter 2, provides an historical context for the review as well as placing it within its contemporary setting. The second part, chapter 3, discusses the definition of power and empowerment, developing a framework for the remaining further sections of the report. The third part, chapter 4, which constitutes the major part of the report, covers the experience of estate regeneration across a number of sectors of community activity – housing, employment and enterprise, social consumption and quality of life, as well as what the authors term 'estate-wide regeneration'. This chapter describes a number of relevant initiatives in each of these fields and asks how far they contribute to empowerment. Chapter 5 returns to the definition of power and empowerment and draws out the implications from the review as a whole for understanding the processes and problems inherent in the empowerment of residents on estates.

THE HISTORICAL CONTEXT AND THE CONTEMPORARY ENVIRONMENT

The history of empowerment in disadvantaged communities goes back to the mutual aid traditions of previous centuries, from which building societies, housing associations and workers' cooperatives emerged, both for production and consumption. Similarly, the history of estates of social housing in the industrial world goes back at least as far as the Bournevilles, New Earswicks and Saltaires, built by philanthropic industrialists seeking to create a less brutalising environment than the slums created by rapidly expanding industry.

Local authorities were given a duty to provide housing after the First World War, but it was after the Second World War that local authority provision rapidly expanded, spurred on by two distinct influences. The first was the devastation caused by the war and the urgent need for a programme of slum clearance. At the same time, the growth of industrialised house-building techniques, together with a town planning system that favoured the separation of residential and industrial land uses, encouraged new development away from traditional locations. The transfer of significant populations to new estates with few facilities and away from their traditional social networks led to the growth of tenants' associations tackling social, adult education and housing management issues. The formation of what was to become the Association of London Housing Estates took place in 1957 (Goetschius, 1969).

The ethos was very much one of self-help, based on education and social work (Thomas, 1983). Most support was directed at improving organisational skills, although Goetschius also identifies "lack of co-operation from authorities" as an issue. There was a growing awareness, however, that poverty had not been abolished despite the advent of the welfare state, and a recognition of the geographical concentration of 'deprivation' was to lead over the next decade to the establishment of central government programmes targeting 'deprived' areas and, at the same time, to a growing politicisation of community organisation.

Central government initiatives, building on the American War on Poverty, drew on ideas relating to the cycle of deprivation and the culture of poverty. The model was pathological, emphasising the failure of individuals or families to cope with poverty, disadvantage or alienation. Empowerment, as embodied in the Educational Priority Areas (EPA), the Urban Programme, the Seebohm report on the personal social services (1968), and the Community Development Projects (CDPs), meant helping people to manage their lives better.

This early perspective on community development was to be challenged, however, by more structural interpretations of disadvantage. As they developed, the CDPs, and less explicitly the Inner Area Studies, offered an analysis that stressed the cumulative effects of economic restructuring and the ineffectiveness of local solutions in the face of national and international forces. The CDPs advocated a conflict model with the objective of redistributing power.

Government, despite its discomfort with the power analysis developed by the government-sponsored CDPs, was eventually to accept an analysis that recognised that the failure of programmes to reach disadvantaged communities was structural rather than pathological. However, the structures initially identified as being at fault by central government were those of the locality. The initiatives of the late 1960s and early 1970s were based on assumptions of systems failure and were characterised by a drive towards improved management and coordination of public services, together with an increased interest in participation (the latter often area-based). Thus the EPAs, the CDPs, and the early Urban Programme, were accompanied or followed by the Skeffington report (1969), General Improvement Area and Housing Action Area legislation, Comprehensive Community Programmes, the Inner Area Studies, and Area Management trials.

This period had three particular features. The first was the rapid growth of a public sector characterised by complex, professionally-based and bureaucratic institutions, with all their attendant failings. Participation was seen as a remedy for some of these dysfunctions (Boaden et al, 1982). Secondly, the large-scale developments of the post-war period in public housing, road building and urban renewal made planning and redevelopment issues the obvious focus of participation initiatives and of increasing community resistance

(Gyford, 1976). Finally, a strong and organised labour movement still existed at that time and workplace struggles tended to eclipse other forms of social action. Although new social identities were emerging, organisation around class remained dominant.

The 1960s had seen growing political awareness around class and social issues. Housing legislation in the early 1970s sparked a series of rent strikes and the oil crisis of 1973 signalled an end to the economic prosperity that had provided the backdrop for early community development and participation initiatives. There was growing resistance to the large-scale planning developments of post-war years and the emerging CDP analysis encouraged conflict models of community action.

During a period when organised protest movements and trade union struggles were at their height, the state needed to reestablish its legitimacy. Participation became an important strategy for sustaining administrative stability and incorporating potentially troublesome elements (Dearlove, 1974; Craig, 1989; Cohen, 1985). Policies to coordinate local service delivery and to encourage participation, however, were still more geared to social engineering than to encouraging local democracy (Hambleton and Taylor, 1993; Gyford, 1976). Empowerment as such was scarcely on the agenda. Meanwhile, community workers who were disenchanted with conflict models looked instead to models of social planning, whereby they worked to sensitise unresponsive systems to the community (Henderson, 1983; Twelvetrees, 1983).

A further wave of government-initiated participation or empowerment emerged with the new Urban Left in the late 1970s and early 1980s, in response to increasing pressure from the new Thatcher government. Local government decentralisation brought with it a new series of area-based initiatives, with smaller units, such as neighbourhoods, as the focus for both service reorganisation and public participation (Hoggett and Hambleton, 1987). Voluntary sector grants strategies (exemplified above all by the policies of the Greater London Council [GLC]) were expanded to encourage the growth of community-based organisations. Along with the creation of race units and women's units, such grant strategies attempted to generate forms of participation that directly reflected new identities of race, gender and sexuality, rather than the homogenised identity of class, for which the concept of 'the council estate' or 'the area of multiple deprivation' had traditionally been used as a proxy.

The philosophy of this phase of community development was political and ideological rather than managerial, and was driven as much by conflicts between central and local government as by community empowerment. Thus, anti-racist and anti-sexist policies were developed within a wider 'rainbow coalition' model of opposition politics, while radical decentralisation initiatives were seen as a strategy for mobilising working class communities in defence of public services against perceived Conservative attacks (Burns, Hambleton and Hoggett, 1994).

To some, 'equality' strategies were seen as encouraging the fragmentation of urban communities. Meekosha (1993) argues that community work over the 1980s was developing into "a mode of work in which ever more tightly delineated minorities and sectors of society experiencing discrimination are channelled into organising the provision of specific, usually volunteer-operated, services", or sucked into participation structures where their separate interests were highly vulnerable to manipulation (Taylor, 1995). At the same time, area-based decentralisation and participation strategies faced the opposite problem of colluding with the exclusion of such groups altogether (Khan, 1989; Burns, Hambleton and Hoggett, 1994). More often than not the privileging of geographical communities through the neighbourhood seemed to exclude those groups who drew their identity from other sources. Community of place dominated community of interest.

Central and local government funding to the voluntary sector as a whole doubled in real terms between 1979 and 1987. Programmes such as the Urban Programme and the Community Programme and smaller initiatives, including Opportunities for Volunteering and the Voluntary Service Unit's Developing Local Voluntary Action Programmes, along with a variety of self-help support schemes, provided a boost to community action and development. In addition, local authorities across the country were employing or funding community development. From the mid-1970s new programmes to create jobs and training opportunities offered a further source of direct support and an opportunity to employ and manage staff for the first time, particularly to groups such as ethnic minority organisations, who still had little access to mainstream budgets.

The capacity was growing in some communities to engage in estate regeneration. However, the problems that they faced had been changing since the mid-1970s. The rationalisation of industry and economic recession hit public housing estates particularly hard as traditional industries declined. Urban policy began to move away from programmes of social regeneration to a focus on wealth creation and economic development, which favoured investment on the large scale (Cooper, Evans and Snaith, 1991) and often bypassed indigenous communities altogether (Hausner, 1991).   Access to jobs was increasingly seen as the route to empowerment.

Nonetheless, other opportunities for empowerment were emerging through a new central government thrust, which was particularly relevant to estate regeneration.   This was the encouragement of the physical – and hopefully social – fabric of housing estates through major regeneration initiatives focusing upon specific estates rather than housing in general. The Priority Estates Project (PEP) introduced in 1979, its incorporation into Estate Action in the mid-1980s, the development of City Challenge in England and the Urban Partnerships in Scotland, and most recently the Single Regeneration Budget offered new potential for community involvement in regeneration.

How empowering these mechanisms were depended on the commitment of public authorities and other outside agencies as well as on the confidence and organising capacity of local communities. However, the power of local authorities themselves was being circumscribed. A series of measures within housing policy sought to empower residents more directly through market mechanisms:

- by making them owners rather than tenants (the sale of council houses);

- by seeking to establish a variety of landlords (encouragement of housing associations and cooperatives and later Housing Action Trusts {HATs]);

- by offering a range of rights to tenants (with respect to repairs, and so on).

Tenant participation and tenant control were encouraged through support for estate management boards and tenant management cooperatives, while community-based housing associations grew in Scotland. Some of these measures were new, while others built on legislation to encourage housing associations and tenant management cooperatives in the 1970s. Along with these incentives there also came a number of requirements. From 1979, when Housing Investment Programmes were introduced as a basis for housing finance, resources for public sector housing were increasingly tight, except where special programmes such as Estate Action were introduced, sometimes through top-slicing existing budgets.

These housing policies reflected more general moves to limit the powers of the local (though not the national) state and to empower people as consumers rather than as citizens. The emphasis in recent years has been on privatisation, greater quality assurance and increased accountability for public services. Although there is still bottom-up pressure for participation, the primary impetus is top-down, focused on management systems, and geared to the individual rather than collective involvement. Thus, from the perspective of central government, empowerment is seen in terms of the ability of individual consumers or their proxy purchasers to participate in the public service marketplace. The concept of citizenship has been blunted and diluted (Du Guy and Salaman, 1992) and a new language has emerged that sees public participation as a method of discharging one's responsibilities and obligations to society rather than as a vehicle for articulating rights and needs (Croft and Beresford, 1992). This, together with the culture of blame that surrounds people with little power in society (eg, one-parent families, benefit claimants) echoes some of the earliest thinking on urban regeneration in the 1960s, which emphasised pathology and the need for individuals to 'stand on their own two feet'. With privatisation, the opportunity has also arisen for communities to become providers; but they take their place in a system where the interest of the citizen and the public sphere have been replaced by a vacuum.

Issues arising from the historical review

This brief historical review has charted a journey in which empowerment has been defined in a number of different ways. From an emphasis on 'deprivation', community pathology and the need for communities to 'heal themselves', explanations of area-based deprivation and how to tackle them have encompassed:

- the need for structural measures and the redistribution of power

- the lack of coordination of services and the need for social engineering

- the need to defend local democracy and local services

- the need to create jobs

- the need to replace state-based systems of allocation with market-based systems.

Two main conclusions can be drawn. Firstly, the shifting nature of ideologies and values over the post-war period has produced new definitions and interpretations of the challenges facing communities and the nature of empowerment. Central to these are the move towards individual choice and the market in local goods and services. The importance of a collective interest, as implied by the terms community and citizenship, has diminished as individual, collective and public rights, duties and responsibilities are redefined. Changes in government policy both reflect and stimulate this reappraisal of the nature of citizen power.

Secondly, there are strong indications of the disempowerment of communities. This stems from the failure of many of the mechanisms of 'filter down' that over the years have been expected to benefit disadvantaged individuals and communities. Programmes providing support to wealth creation and choice have failed to spread downwards through the system. Although there have been significant changes in the structure of housing and labour markets, there is evidence of a continuing, indeed increasing, polarisation and marginalisation of those unable to benefit from structural change and an attempt to cast them as the sources of their own disadvantage. Recent work underlines the growing gap between rich and poor and the growing concentration of poverty on particular groups and areas (Joseph Rowntree Foundation, 1995). As employment and housing markets become increasingly segmented, the disadvantaged find it more difficult to gain access to resources and to market position. Loss of material power is compounded by the fragmentation of communities, of power, and of institutions. There is a further potential for loss of power as community interests are 'sucked in' to formal structures, and what have hitherto been radical and distinctive interests are incorporated.

Before moving into the main body of the report it is important to stress that it is increasingly impossible to discuss the locality in isolation from external pressures. The community development literature has always recognised the location of 'community' within a broader framework of analysis, but it seems that it has become even more important than hitherto to understand the problems of local communities within a city-wide, national and global context, as well as in the context of locality, neighbourhood and estate.

These three tendencies – the emergence of new definitions of community and power, the disempowerment of increasingly marginalised communities, and the need to set the local within a broader socio-economic context – all underlie the analysis of estate-based community empowerment that follows.

Key issues in chapter

3

DEFINITIONS AND INTERPRETATIONS OF EMPOWERMENT

Concepts of power

This report does not seek to explore the theoretical definitions of power in any depth. Rather, it is the authors' wish to emphasise the conceptual difficulties inherent in examining power and empowerment and the considerations that need to be addressed before particular strategies can be evaluated.

It is apparent from the authors' review that in the literature of participation and involvement there is surprisingly little explicit discussion of 'power', even if the idea of empowerment is implied in many of the participation studies. Croft and Beresford (1992) point out, however, that empowerment is not synonymous with the practice of participation, and they argue for a more explicit analysis of power. They draw attention to the three classic dimensions of power (Lukes, 1974):

- the overt resolution of conflict between two or more conflicting positions

- the covert or hidden dimension that excludes issues from public decision making

- the third structural dimension of through which interests are institutionalised within society, and structures of power are accepted and internalised without question or even recognition.

The issue of what gets onto the agenda for discussion and what is excluded (Lukes, 1974; Bachrach and Baratz, 1962) is central to community empowerment. Though posed in terms of theory this is an extremely practical question. The question from communities is, so often, 'why can't we talk about X' – an issue that authority has excluded from debate.

A different question is whether power is finite and held by particular people or groups or whether it is an infinite resource open to all to grasp. Does (resident) empowerment involve taking power from others (elected politicians, professionals, etc) or simply increasing the amount of power that is available? Croft and Beresford (1992) argue that empowerment is not a zero-sum game and that power can be taken by some without reducing the power of others. Holmes (1992) also argues that empowerment is a positive-sum experience and that empowerment means enabling people to take action. Such an interpretation of power invites comparison with the theoretical position of Foucault (1980), who argues that it is open to any actor to take power by engaging in discourse about what can or cannot be done. In this sense almost any measure of participation or resident engagement might be regarded as empowering insofar as it allows those who lack power to make an input to the renegotiation of the terms of social or political relationships between community and authority.   An alternative view is that power is more readily understood as a finite resource. In this view, empowerment for some means disempowerment for others and the dilution of existing power structures.   In this analysis empowerment implies that a shift of power is needed from authority to community and that politicians and professionals accept in explicit terms the need to let go or give up power.

Equally important is an understanding of organisational power and of the way in which power within large institutions is distributed according to professional or managerial norms, which restrict its flow and effectively concentrate power in relatively few hands.   This analogy suggests that power is not possessed but flows through circuits (Clegg, 1989). Developing this image, switches may need to be thrown to remove blockages, or new linkages developed to allow power to flow in new ways and around new circuits.

Finally, and most crucially, debates on empowerment need also to understand the barriers that exclude individual people from engaging in any kind of social life, let alone processes of empowerment. Maslow's hierarchy of needs (Maslow, 1954) draws attention to the powerlessness brought about by the absence of the basic material requirements of human existence: shelter, work, income, services, and so on. Psychological and labelling theories (Seligman, 1975; Tajfel,

1981; Servian, 1993; Taylor, Kestenbaum and Symons, 1976) highlight the lack of confidence, the stigmatisation and the sense of personal failure that accompany material, political and educational disadvantage and create barriers that are rarely understood by more powerful actors.

There is widespread evidence in the literature of a concentration of poverty arising from extreme disadvantage in the labour market and in the markets that have now been created in welfare services (Joseph Rowntree Foundation, 1995; Power, 1994). This is compounded by lack of transport, an inhospitable environment, impoverished and expensive local shops and a negative image in the eyes of the outside world. Ultimately this leads to feelings of personal inadequacy and failure, often reinforced by a pathology of disadvantage that fails to place individual circumstances within their structural context and emphasises the significance of Lukes' third face of power.

The dimensions of empowerment

In looking at the strategies adopted for empowerment in estate regeneration, four related dimensions are identified, along which empowerment can be understood. These build on an analysis developed through research on community care for the Joseph Rowntree Foundation (Taylor et al, 1992) and across service areas for the Local Government Management Board (LGMB) (Gaster and Taylor, 1993).

- the *processes* of empowerment (how?)

- the extent or *degree* of empowerment (how much?)

- the *focus* of empowerment (where?)

- the *ownership* of empowerment (who?)

The processes of empowerment

Hirschman (1970) differentiated two different approaches to empowerment as 'exit' and 'voice'. Exit is the idea that drives policies seeking to give consumers more choice or the chance to opt out of a given system of delivery. It allows individual consumers to go elsewhere if they do not like the particular provider on offer.

However, dissatisfied consumers may not wish to (or indeed be able to) go elsewhere. In that case, voice is the mechanism through which consumers and citizens can seek to change existing services and the way they are run. Many commentators would argue that a mixture of both is the ideal. To what extent do estate regeneration programmes offer exit and voice? Do residents start from a position where they have the power of exit to alternative services? And how does that affect their perception of power?

Residents may opt for Hirschman's third dimension ('loyalty'), whereby they accept passively what is on offer. Alternatively, they may become alienated – a fourth dimension that Lowery, de Hoog and Lyons (1992) added to Hirschman's framework, calling it 'neglect'. To what extent do estate regeneration programmes actively engage residents across the board, and what are the processes through which such engagement is facilitated? Conversely, what are the barriers that inhibit empowerment?

Finally, residents can adopt these different strategies as individuals or through collective mechanisms. Rioting may be seen as collective alienation, opting out as collective exit, complaints procedures as individual voice, and so on (see Figure 1, p 15). It is important to recognise that collective action can be a means to individual empowerment, and vice versa. Alternatively, collective empowerment can deny power to others through exclusion. One individual's empowerment can also deny empowerment to another (eg, the 'Right to Buy' could be said to have decreased the access and choice available to those who cannot afford to buy). Which of these strategies are being adopted on estates, and does power for some empower or exclude others?

The degree or extent of empowerment

Residents can be given (or take) varying degrees of power – as expressed in ladders or scales of participation, such as those initially developed by Arnstein (1969). At the bottom of such a ladder (see Figure 2, p 16), they are merely informed or even manipulated. At the top they are given control. How far up such ladders have estate regeneration programmes gone?

Figure 1:   Processes of empowerment

Note: individual responses are shown in the diamond; collective responses are shown outside the diamond.

Source: Adapted from Lowery, de Hoog and Lyons (1992)

Figure 2:   Arnstein's ladder of participation

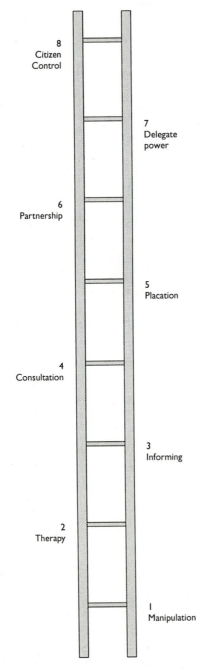

Source: Arnstein (1969)

Such ladders assume that more control is better than less control. If people have the resources to make use of the control this may be so, but handing over responsibility and control against people's wishes or without the resources and skills that are needed can set people up for failure. This may be one reason why residents have not always voted for control even when it has been offered. What assistance have estate regeneration programmes offered people to allow them to exercise more power rather than simply taking on responsibility? And how far do those exercising control share power with others on the estate who use their services?

Nor is there any step on the ladder at which empowerment can be said to have been achieved. Even the top of a ladder of empowerment cannot be seen as the summit of achievement. Many residents do not wish to be collectively empowered or involved, to participate, or to climb a ladder. Indeed, it has been a weakness of many participation exercises to assume that everyone should be involved. Further, an assumption that users are in control begs the question of which users are in control, what power they grant to others and how a particular user-run service or initiative fits in with the wider pattern of estate regeneration. Does it exclude? Does it offer choices to others? Does it reinforce or conflict with other initiatives?

The focus of empowerment

Residents can have power as consumers in the selection and use of a particular service, or they can have power as citizens over the range of services that are available to them (eg, through planning mechanisms) and the rights they have to those services. They may again exercise this power as individuals or through collective mechanisms. On which of these points do estate regeneration programmes focus? How far do they give people a say in all aspects of their lives and how far do they allow empowerment at different points in the planning and delivery of services and jobs?

There has been considerable concern in recent years over the way in which consumer empowerment is displacing citizen empowerment and the rights of citizenship. Collective voice in the range of services on offer empowers residents as citizens, recognising interests, rights and responsibilities beyond their individual consumer interest. Currently, the policy emphasis is on individual services. How far do estate regeneration programmes empower people as citizens?

The ownership of empowerment

Residents have many different relationships with services as consumers. They may be primary or secondary users, using a service themselves or associated with someone else's use of a service (as a parent or carer, for example). They may be paying for a service, using a service that is free to all as of right, or using a rationed service that is free to only those who are assessed as in need of it. They may wish to use a service but have no access to it or they may be past or potential users. They may be compelled to use a service sectioned under the 1983 Mental Health Act, for example, or unwillingly affected by someone else's use of a service. This not only demonstrates the different interests that residents hold in different parts of the life or services on an estate – it also illustrates crucially that interests may overlap and conflict. How do estate regeneration programmes deal with the range of different interests on an estate? How, in particular, do new approaches to consumer empowerment – estate contracts and agreements, for example – contribute to community empowerment?

It is essential to ask how far power is spread. Does it lie simply with an elite group or a particular section of the population? Is it used to exclude? How have issues of discrimination been dealt with? Is it confined to the most vocal? What ways have been found of engaging people at the different levels at which they feel able to engage? What have been the mechanisms through which views have been channelled? Throughout the history of attempts to empower people, the issue of representation has been problematic, used to channel views but criticised by power holders and residents alike when, not surprisingly, diverse views cannot be squeezed into a form acceptable to outsiders. Where is representation appropriate and how can it be made to work?

Putting it all together

There is no 'right way' of empowering that can be constructed from these dimensions. Empowerment has to be seen as a cycle or as a continuous learning process, and evaluated in terms of its continuity, its distribution, its sustainability and the extent to which it builds more general capacity across communities.

This section has raised questions about what power is and how it might work. It has then looked at the processes by which policies seek to 'em-power' and people seek to take power. These processes start from a position where people are excluded from the job market and deprived of services. This exclusion leads to a sense of personal inadequacy and failure, often reinforced by a culture that blames the victim and stereotypes isolated areas of disadvantage. To change this, whether one sees power as something that is possessed and hoarded or something that flows and becomes blocked, requires that people first be given basic levels and standards of service to get beyond the struggle to meet basic needs. After this there are both individual and collective routes to power. Individually, people can make their own choices about the jobs and services they require and policy can help to make those choices become available. They can decide to exit collectively from the public services on offer. They can passively accept what is on offer or become alienated. Or they can choose to have collective voice, and once more policy and their own preferences can determine what degree of power they are given or can take, to the point of owning or managing their own services. Collective voice can also be exercised in strategies that seek to address the quality of life on the estate as a whole (as opposed to particular services) and this may involve people who have chosen individual routes to service or economic empowerment as well as those who have taken collective routes.

4

THE EXPERIENCE OF ESTATE REGENERATION

This chapter considers how the processes discussed earlier have been implemented, and what has been learned about their operation in three broad areas:

- housing tenure and management

- employment, enterprise and income

- social and environmental regeneration.

In each section the authors draw on existing literature to consider basic rights, whether the routes to empowerment have been individual or collective, whether they are offered through exit or voice, and what degree of power has been extended to or taken by people on estates. The final section moves to a more holistic view of estate-wide partnership initiatives, and their potential to give people power over the total pattern of services and opportunities on estates.

Housing

Housing is central to estate regeneration. It is housing need that brings many people onto an estate, and on many peripheral estates the housing office is often the first point of contact, whatever the problem. Housing authorities are still responsible for the whole neighbourhood and are therefore in a position to have a better strategic awareness than most other departments or agencies dealing with the estate, although this may change with increased diversification of tenure. Much multi-purpose estate action, whether it is initiated by tenants or outside agencies, has its origins in action on housing. Hausner (1991) suggests that one reason for this is that housing development can command relatively large budgets.

Housing has also been at the centre of central government policies to reform public service delivery. For several years now 'simply sitting tight' has not been an option for housing authorities (Duncan, 1989). They are expected to diversify tenure in order to increase choice, and to devolve the housing management function.

Access and standards

Council estates exist to give people access to housing, but this housing has often been of a poor quality, poorly maintained and poorly managed. In the past, residualisation of council estates has been encouraged by the 'sink estate' mentalities of many housing authorities and by the dumping of what were perceived as 'problem families'. Tenure diversification can make an enormous contribution to estate regeneration, to improved standards and to renewed confidence in the estate and its communities. Paradoxically, however, policies for tenure diversification may lead some public housing estates, built originally to extend access to quality affordable housing and to rehouse families from the appalling conditions of the slums, to become, instead, the accommodation of last resort for those who have no choice. Even housing associations, encouraged to become alternative providers of social housing, are finding that pressures to become more efficient in the market are forcing them to concentrate those least able to afford housing choice on larger estates (Page, 1994). Equally, where housing investment and better management focus on some parts, but not all of an estate, there is a danger of polarisation between the regenerated and the unimproved areas of the estate.

A range of initiatives have been put into motion to improve both the quality (through targeted investment programmes, such as Action on Estates), and the management of estates (through decentralisation initiatives, as originally in Walsall) (Seabrook, 1984), and subsequently more widely stimulated, for example, through the PEP programmes (Power, 1984; Gregory and White, 1991). These can include local allocations policies, but seldom do. Decentralisation initiatives have mainly been concerned with local delivery and, with the exception of PEP, do not necessarily promote community participation. ⌐ Priority Estates Project

Successive PEP and other surveys have found the decentralisation (ie, local delivery) of housing management services to give increased satisfaction to tenants (Power, 1987; Gregory and White, 1991; Holmes, 1992; Glennerster and Turner, 1993). Decentralisation of delivery does not in itself redistribute power, but locally-based repairs systems, local caretaking and lettings policies can all result in faster response rates and policies geared to the needs of the particular locality. Easier access to housing officers on their own territory may give tenants more confidence and hence more individual power. The empowerment of front-line staff is itself an important first step to the empowerment of service users (Power, 1992; Gaster and Taylor, 1993). Demoralised and undervalued staff are unlikely to give a good service. The PEP model is reproduced below.

Figure 3:   The PEP model

The PEP model
A full-time local office, responsible for repairs, lettings and allocations, rents and benefits, housing advice and empty properties
A local repairs team able to handle emergency, day-to-day and void repairs and planned and cyclical maintenance
Resident caretakers, responsible to the local manager
Tenant consultation and participation in the management and improvement of the estate
An estate budget under the direct control of the estate manager
On-going training for staff and residents
Monitoring of performance
Coordination of other services to the estate

Source: Zipfel (1989)

Empowerment through 'exit'

Collective 'exit' can be exercised through tenants' choice initiatives. These allow tenants to vote for another landlord, with the added incentive in some areas of the increased investment, of a HAT. The latter option has been enhanced following its early failures through guarantees on rent levels and the opportunity to transfer ownership back to the local authority without costs accruing.

Individual exit has been made easier through Right to Buy, which allows individuals to move out of local authority tenure and may also give them the option to move away from the estate altogether. As Power (1994) points out, owner occupation in society is the tenure associated with success; subsidies and discounts favour owner occupation, for those who have the wherewithal. Some authorities have given tenants the further option to exit through Tenants' Incentive Schemes, where they are given money to enable them to buy. Other policies seek to increase the range of tenure options available on the estate. Action on Estates offers incentives to local authorities to create sales zones and shared ownership schemes or to float off provision to housing associations. This has been a major feature of The Scottish Office Urban Partnership initiatives, with the disposal of council stock and the construction of new build combining to reduce the near total monopoly position of the local authority.

Choice of tenure offers genuine opportunities for the individual and for communities. If tenants do not like the service offered, they can go elsewhere, as individuals or as a group; but not everyone wants or can afford the responsibilities of owner occupation. A more mixed tenure base within an estate does, however, bring benefits for all, by improving the population mix and potentially bringing more skills, income and self-esteem onto the estate (Holmes, 1992).

However, the evidence suggests that tenure change is not a priority for many who already live on estates. The initial attempts to bring in tenants' choice backfired because they galvanised previously inactive tenants to resist moves, based on an unfair voting system, to take away their existing tenancy conditions. One reason may have been fears about security of tenure under a private landlord. Others see their actions as an endorsement of the council as landlord:

> The dominant view of council tenants, propelled forward by government policy is of an oppressed, dissatisfied minority eagerly searching for exit routes out of the tenure. But surveys of council tenants have consistently shown levels of satisfaction with service of which most banks and building societies would be proud. (Cole and Smith, 1993)

Where public housing has been levered out of local authority control, the evidence is that it has been done through a heavy investment of funds. It is unlikely that the HATs that have now been set up will be allowed to fail, but how generalisable their experience as 'flagships' will be remains to be seen. The Stockbridge Village Trust, for example, achieved improvements after considerable investment that would not be replicable generally (Penn, 1987), and there is unlikely to be money for future initiatives of this magnitude (Zipfel, 1989). Page's research on housing associations (1994) suggests that housing management problems may be the product of large estates with an unbalanced population rather than of the local authority as a landlord, but with tenure diversification usually being allied to physical improvement it is hard to distinguish the impact of one or the other factor in increasing housing satisfaction.

Empowerment through 'voice'

Tenants' charters and other consumer initiatives are giving tenants access to individual voice through satisfaction surveys and feedback cards, surveys and improved complaints procedures (Gaster and Taylor, 1993). Though offering the right of redress, many of these charters are devised from above. Tenants rarely have a voice in determining these standards and they operate after the event, rather than building in quality from the beginning (Gaster and Taylor, 1993). There is no guarantee that action will be taken across the board where quality is defective rather than just in those cases where the tenant has the confidence and the knowledge to complain. Experience of surveys has repeatedly shown that satisfaction depends on expectations. Demoralised tenants on stigmatised council estates are likely to have low expectations.

Current policies offer many opportunities for the exercise of collective voice. These vary according to the amount of power housing authorities are willing to cede, whether the initiative is taken by them or by tenants, and at what point in the housing service tenants wish to exercise some degree of control. Using Arnstein's ladder as a model (see p 16), the initial steps have taken the form of information (sometimes as a public relations exercise, proposals sent out for comment or public meetings on selected aspects of housing policy). All these are forms of top-down consultation and are entirely at the discretion of the authority (Gaster and Taylor, 1993). They do not require collective action, although a collective response is likely to carry more weight than an individual one. However, the literature documents many examples of tenants taking the initiative to influence policy through campaigns on different aspects of housing policy.

Over time, more and more authorities have taken action to set up more formal participation mechanisms, which offer a range of influence to tenants and may be tied into the formal political process through area-based tenant management subcommittees (although this is more difficult since the 1989 Local Government and Housing Act prevented the cooption of voting members). The PEP model (p 22) demands not only decentralisation of housing management but the involvement of tenants through active encouragement of tenant activity and opportunities for involvement in decision making. These opportunities may be in the form of an estate committee or, more recently, through the creation of an Estate Management Board (EMB), with tenants in the majority but sharing responsibility with the authority.

Glennerster and Turner (1993) argue that voice, though difficult to implement well and theoretically less effective a form of pressure than exit, is the only realistic option for deprived estates. Most tenants cannot afford to buy and far from acting as an incentive for better service, the exercise of exit options is likely to limit options for the rest.

Tenants' voice may be forced on an authority from below, allowed in from above, or positively encouraged from above. The case-study literature over the years is rich with stories of campaigns by tenants for rehabilitation, improved heating, the removal of dampness and better facilities, with recourse on occasion to the courts (see, for example, Craig, 1980; Henderson, Wright and Wyncoll, 1982; Taylor and Presley, 1987; Smith, 1993). It also underlines the importance of community development support in building the capacity and confidence for tenants to exercise their voice.

Studies of community action (Smith, 1993) have found that many tenants' organisations start in response to some grievance that gives them momentum and inspires a high degree of participation. This means that many start with an oppositional or confrontational stance. Thereafter they may settle down to a more 'realistic' or negotiated relationship with those in power – a kind of 'trade union' role of advocacy and bargaining on behalf of the membership (Cairncross, Clapham and Goodlad, 1992). Alternatively, they may move into the management of social facilities or other services (Frankenberg, 1966; Goetschius, 1969). Some choose, however, to remain outside the system, for fear of being incorporated by the state or being sucked into formal consultation arrangements based on an agenda and rules of engagement set by the authority, which often serve to take resident representatives further and further away from their constituency (Taylor, Newcastle and Sheffield Tenants' Federation, 1986).

Nonetheless, knocking against a closed door can prove highly frustrating and wasteful of energy.   Cairncross, Clapham and Goodlad (1992) found a highly significant association between formal arrangements for tenant participation on the part of authorities and the existence of tenants' associations. The agitational role was, not surprisingly, most likely where tenants' groups continued to receive no support from the local authority.

Tenants may become involved in many different aspects of housing and one area where tenant involvement has been particularly imaginative and successful at involving the range of tenants has been in housing design (Gibson, 1993; Lusk, 1988; Watson, 1994). Design is tangible and visible and lends itself to direct participation across a wide front (see pp 50-54). Duncan (1989) warns, however, that the prospects for tenant involvement in housing association design are diminishing as housing association rules on procurement push them into building on standardised models.

Experience of more formal involvement of tenants, through area management committees or even estate committees (Dale and Derricourt, 1989) has varied according to the degree of power accorded to tenants. Such committees remain tied to the culture and mechanisms of local government. Early evaluations of the PEP criticised housing management for failing to delegate enough powers either to estate offices or to tenants themselves. An increasingly important element of the PEP model has been formal and effective involvement in decision making.

Local budgets, in particular, have been seen as the key to local control. However, evaluation of the PEP projects (Zipfel, 1989) suggested that:

- decision-making powers and the degree of tenant involvement were often limited and style and content of meetings was dictated by the local authority;

- few projects could identify and establish estate revenue budgets;

- control over non-housing services continued to present problems;

- it was difficult for local authorities to sustain a high interest in one estate over a long period of time;

- the model was vulnerable to change dictated from the centre (eg, staff cuts across the authority, which did not take account of local priorities).

The result was that PEP recommended the adoption of EMBs that gave tenants more control. Evaluating EMBs, Dickson and Robertson (1993) found that success requires "good information, adequate servicing of committees, not too much channelling through committees, and tenants able to initiate spending". The transition from full council control needs to be carefully planned with adequate support and training, and Dickson and Robertson warn that short cuts at the development stage may have major costs later.

Department of the Environment (DoE) funding regimes have posed major problems. For example, the Hornsey Lane EMB, which was a trailblazer, had money for 18 months to employ a housing development worker, but found that the process took two-and-a-half years (Spray, 1992). It was the first grant of its kind and the forms were overwhelming, with major delays in decision making on the part of the authorities. An evaluation of this EMB (Spray, 1992) suggested that it worked because it was small and already employed its own community workers – it allowed the physical state to be transformed through rehabilitation and it had local authority support and experience. These lessons may equally apply as tenants move to take more control.

Collective control

Tenant Management Cooperatives (TMCs) move people further up the ladder to a position where tenants have full responsibility for management but where ownership still resides with the local authority. Legislation to allow local authorities to hand over some or all of their responsibilities to TMCs was introduced by the Labour government in 1975.

Various forms of owner cooperatives represent full ownership, although only those which are fully mutual must have all tenants in membership and only have tenants in membership. Non-mutual cooperatives and community-based housing associations occupy a spectrum between the fully mutual and a housing association still centred on a particular area, but where tenants may not be in the majority. All these forms of tenant ownership are more common in Scotland than elsewhere in Britain, especially on estates.

The cooperative sector remains a minority sector, even in Scotland, where a combination of high levels of public housing with imaginative responses to the challenges of public expenditure cuts has given rise to a stronger tradition (Clapham and Kintrea, 1992). Recent policy developments, however, offer the prospect of growth across the UK. The Estate Action programme has given the formation of tenant management cooperatives in particular a new impetus in England and a growing number of local authorities may find, like their Scottish counterparts before them, that they offer one of the more promising avenues for keeping housing in social ownership under the control of tenants.

Evaluations of cooperatives have included everything from EMBs to owner cooperatives, and it is not easy to tease out the lessons of each type. Many of the problems they face and lessons they have learnt are similar, but tenants may prefer to stay with the idea of an EMB, where the responsibility for the estate is shared. Many tenants are suspicious about tenant control (Duncan, 1989); even in Glasgow, where this form of tenure has been most successful, tenants were initially resistant (Clapham and Kintrea, 1992). More power also means more responsibility and more work. Tenants of estates that appear to be facing huge problems may be wary of "taking on the task of turning around a severely depressed estate" on their own (Smith, 1993). It is possible that "tenant management schemes, rather than providing solutions to deep-seated problems, may simply expose to tenants, more graphically than their council was ever able to, the nature of current financial under provision for council housing" (Smith, 1993). On the other hand, TMCs are less vulnerable than EMBs to council-initiated changes, since they have a wider brief. They also have more control over their budget.

In comparison with the local authority, McRafferty and Riley (1989) find that, on balance, cooperatives provide a more satisfactory management service and are "able to meet needs for better housing and improved participation in management by providing a small-scale, personalised, locally-based and effective management service at a competitive cost", although they found that housing association TMCs had the least satisfactory results. Again, it is possible to argue that the advantages of cooperatives may have as much to do with size as with who the landlord is – many TMCs have also had considerable support from local authorities.

Several authors point to the familiar problem that the majority of the work of both EMBs and cooperatives falls on few people, although mechanisms such as street representation may bring new tenants into active participation.   Duncan (1989) suggests that the larger the cooperative, the lower the number of active members.   McRafferty, Riley and the DoE (1989) suggest that participation can be a problem once cooperatives are up and running, although some case-study evidence suggests that this may not be inevitable.

Some cooperatives and EMBs tackle the problems of participation and capacity by selecting people on the basis of their interest in tenant participation and willingness to attend training sessions on tenant management (Watson, 1994).   While this appears to have much to recommend it, it does raise another dilemma.   Will cooperatives empower the most able at the expense of others?   If the only way to get access to resources is to become a joiner, cooperation may be simply another way of moving the line between the empowered and the disempowered down a few notches.   There is the additional danger of exclusion.   Dickson and Robertson (1993) were critical of the lack of attention to equal opportunities in one of the two TMCs they studied.

Low levels of involvement not only affect the amount of work EMBs and cooperatives can take on but may also affect their accountability.   In Hornsey Lane, an active tenants association continued alongside the EMB and offered a parallel channel for influence and accountability (Spray, 1992).

Dickson and Robertson (1993) argue that there is a "need to examine and evaluate ways of increasing the enfranchisement of the majority who may not wish at present to make such an all-embracing commitment to involvement in the running of the estate".   It may be that tenants are always going to feel insufficiently involved, whoever manages.   There is also a tension between the need for experience and the need to bring in new people.   Clapham and Kintrea (1992), acknowledging this problem, ask "whether mass involvement is the appropriate touchstone for judging cooperatives, or whether collective control is sufficient".   They argue that tenants in cooperatives have been proven to be well informed and to have the channels to participate if they wish. The importance of cooperatives is that "the structures for resident involvement exist" (and, one could add, are enshrined in their constitution rather than capable of being taken away at whim) "and can be re-activated when it is thought necessary." (Clapham and Kintrea, 1992).

This raises the question of whether cooperatives do really have control? Clapham and Kintrea (1992) point out that even owner cooperatives may be subject to constraints placed upon them by funders. The motivation behind local authority interest in tenant management cooperatives may be suspect, in that this model may be used to keep the housing in public ownership as opposed to going to another landlord. If this allows local authorities to exert undue control, then this is a problem.

Control also depends on capacity and most writers underline the investment that is required to make a cooperative or an EMB work: "It may take up to five years for many groups of tenants to develop into a fully fledged financial and legal entity with sufficient stability, knowledge and security to gain independence. The drain on the most active and able tenants through many hours of voluntary work can be divisive as a majority sit back and enjoy the fruits of their effort" (Power, 1988b). Even the development of an EMB is a "lengthy and demanding process which requires great stamina of tenants" (Dickson and Robertson, 1993). The move from campaigning to running a service can in itself be a difficult one – a problem that is rarely anticipated. Some authors are concerned that the rewards being offered by central government may lead tenants and/or authorities to embark on a scheme without sufficient long-term commitment and that Compulsory Competitive Tendering (CCT) may further complicate developments by putting undue pressure on time. In these circumstances, TMCs may be set up to fail.

Given that cooperatives do seem to offer the opportunity of empowerment to some tenants, both by offering the possibility of improved housing management and by offering the option to participate in and take control of their housing, what are the prerequisites to their successful development? The literature suggests the following:

- A fertile political environment. Political, practical and financial support from local councils, and more recently central government, has been crucial to the success of cooperatives where they have flourished, especially in Scotland.

- Considerable grass roots pressure.   The high levels of perseverance to make cooperatives work demand a strong impetus from tenants (McRafferty, Riley and the DoE, 1989).

- Professional support (which itself often relies on local government funding) and revenue grants for early development.

- Successful local models from which new cooperatives can learn.

Summary

A range of well-documented options exist in the housing arena for involvement of all kinds, while consumerism has made inroads into the quality of housing management and conditions, insofar as scarce and targeted resources allow. The evidence so far suggests, however, that the potential of exit options is limited. While opportunities for tenant voice in socially-owned housing are increasingly common, the amount of power councils and housing associations are willing to concede is highly variable (Chartered Institute of Housing/Tenant Participation Advisory Service, 1989).   Opportunities for joint management and control are expanding, but relatively slowly and with considerable assistance from local authorities. They remain very much in the minority and how they will be affected by CCT remains to be seen.

Encouraging tenant empowerment requires commitment and resources. Many of the same mistakes are made over and over again and the need to involve more people is a recurring theme. The literature abounds, however, with suggestions as to the principles that are required for effective participation in housing management, at whatever point in the service. Power (1987) offers an effective summary:

Principles of effective participation

- Adequate time-scales.

- Support and training, including community development.

- Resident access to good independent advice.

- Adequate information and clear communication.

- Access to resources that can be controlled locally.

- Real commitment from power holders.

- A willingness to hand over power and to work with residents as equals.

- Results.

- Opportunities for informal as well as formal participation.

- Accountability and controls to prevent abuse.

- The ability to remove an unrepresentative clique.

Employment, enterprise and income

Employment on housing estates is often high, long standing and immune to programmes that aim to integrate residents into the labour market. In many of the peripheral estates of smaller towns as well as the larger cities the local economy has largely disintegrated, dependence on state welfare is high and poverty widespread (Holmes, 1992). In the four Scottish Urban Partnership initiatives (concentrated in major areas of deprivation and disadvantage) there continued to be an increase in the unemployment rate from 1981 to 1991, coupled with a decrease in the economically active population. This produced increased dependency – for every wage earner in each of the four areas there is now more than one non-earner.

The economic circumstances of such estates need to be seen in historical context. Estates never had many local jobs since typically they were residential areas built at a time when segregation of land uses was a major feature of planning practice. Where there were local or nearby jobs there has been extensive job loss as traditional manufacturing activity either disappeared altogether or was rationalised and relocated. With few opportunities for new infrastructure (as compared to inner areas or docklands, for example) there has been limited new job creation. Concentrations of low skill, lack of access to training opportunities, poor access to jobs, and discrimination in recruitment as a result of stereotyping, all contribute to the effective exclusion of the residents of many estates from economic opportunities.

This section discusses first the question of basic employment rights, before turning to the question of individual empowerment through exit or (in this case) personal investment through education and training in the capacities to seek a job elsewhere. The discussion then moves on to collective response and the emergence of local development agencies and community business. Finally, the section shifts from employment and enterprise to the question of non-waged income and addresses issues of access to benefits (often individualised) and of collective empowerment in relation to income.

Access, rights and employment

Basic rights of access to employment do not exist in relation to the labour market – there is no 'right to work'. Thus, empowerment in relation to employment takes the form less of a demand for or negotiation of rights but more of investment in the abilities, skills, capacities and experience that will enable individuals to compete in the labour market. Being without a job is disempowering. Not only does unemployment mean that an individual is without a wage or other payment for work but it also brings a range of other problems – lack of personal confidence and self-esteem, social exclusion (Daniel, 1972; Sinfield, 1970), exclusion from credit, and weakened access to a range of normal services. Long-term unemployment is a major contributory factor towards social and economic marginalisation and exclusion.

The individual in principle has the choice of exit. Elsewhere in Europe (though to a lesser degree in the UK) labour mobility has been a more common feature as young and employable people (usually males) migrate within and beyond national boundaries in search of work. There have been traditional migration flows in Britain notably to the cities and from North to South, and a feature of many of the estates discussed is the fall in population consequent upon the exodus of young people. Thus exit is a real option, but one which can cream estates of skills and enterprise.

Nevertheless, movement is limited, not least by the constraints in the housing market, and estates retain many people. A range of policies, implemented mainly through central (but to a small degree also local) government, from school education, through the post-school period into training, job experience, job search, and recruitment, seek to support individuals. Historically, these services have not been planned or managed on an estate basis but the decentralised offices of the Employment Service are often on or close to an estate with high unemployment, just as social security offices can be on or close to an estate simply because of the distribution of the need or demand for the service. However, there is a long history of the failure of the employment and welfare services to meet adequately the needs of residents on estates with high unemployment and poverty. There is also a history of initiatives, from CDPs onwards, which have sought to protest against the levels of unemployment on such estates, and to campaign for better employment and welfare services.

There remain initiatives that concentrate upon 'voice', but in general (and in the face of recession), the degree of protest about unemployment and the audibility of demands for more jobs has decreased. Thus the Unemployed Centres that characterised many estates in the early 1980s (for example, Meegan, 1989) acted as the focus for protest and action against a series of measures – poll tax, the removal of the Community Programme, cuts in local council services, and tightening of welfare eligibility rules. Many credit unions were the product of that time and employment work concentrated on campaigning for jobs and protesting against closures and against public sector job cuts.

By the early 1990s protest had weakened and estate-based employment work was increasingly focused upon projects that were linked into the programmes of the formal regeneration initiatives. Thus, Task Forces, City Action Teams, Training and Enterprise Councils (TECs), Business Leadership Teams and Business in the Community began to be involved in partnerships of one form or another of which City Challenge in England and Urban Partnerships in Scotland have so far been the most visible. These partnerships began to put pressure upon the statutory agencies to improve their services to disadvantaged estates and urban regeneration policy, and consequently policies impacting upon estates were influenced by the culture of targeting. Thus 'Getting People into Jobs' (Hayton, 1990) and 'Targeting' (Turok and Wannop, 1990) drew attention away from estate-based initiatives and focused it upon the work of TECs, the Employment Service and the recruiting practices of the private sector. In many respects this is potentially an empowering process. Local strengths are recognised (eg, through local skills audits) and linkages built with established sections of the labour market. There is now widespread targeting of training onto the most disadvantaged in the labour market, and access courses, preparation for work, customised training for local firms that commit themselves at least to interview, together with resource intensive placement services are common-place.

Such targeted work is often channelled through new local development agencies funded either by a Partnership, by a city-wide or regional development agency, by a TEC or by a combination of funding from all. There have been successes in these emergent new local economic development agencies (Turok and Wannop, 1990), particularly in relation to training and placement, but their existence is often fragile beyond initial pump priming funding, and their potential for income generation upon which survival may depend is limited. Where such agencies can combine activities and develop a trading arm of some kind (as in the Govan initiative over the years) survival and success is more likely, but some of the most widely known initiatives (eg, Drumchapel) have encountered major difficulties.

Mention places but does not give specific

Investment in renewal of the physical infrastructure of estates normally accounts for the bulk of the resource input. The spin-off from such construction investment into local jobs, however, is minimal (McGregor et al, 1995). The structure of the construction industry, the length and continuity of building contracts, the range of skills required and the tendency for employees or trainees to return to unemployment, all militate against the creation of long-term and lasting employment benefits from the construction elements of estate regeneration.

The relationship with and accountability to local communities also poses problems for local development agencies and community representation can clash with the commercial confidentiality sometimes required in a development agency that will operate as a private company. In Castlemilk, for example, the community withdrew from the Local Development Agency (LDA) because of the latter's perceived lack of accountability to local people.

Community enterprise

Local Development Agencies support training and placement but also direct themselves to local enterprise. It was not until the mid-1980s that two strands of community-based action came together to focus attention upon estate-based economic activity.

First, the PEP, which had hitherto concentrated primarily upon housing management and tenant involvement issues, extended its thinking to consideration of employment (Power, 1988a). Drawing particularly upon Bootstraps, Broadwater Farm and Penrhys, together with ideas on employment creation from 25 management experiments, PEP illustrated the scope for job creation for local residents. A later PEP-supported study (Bootstrap Enterprises and MacFarlane, 1989) examined the feasibility of developing 'One Stop Shop' initiatives on five estates as a means of integrating training, placement and business development activities for estate residents. The recommendations from that report emphasised the variety of routes to improved access to employment for local residents. Two new One Stop Shops were thought appropriate in Hull and Stoke on Trent; on the Birmingham Bloomsbury estate better services from existing providers seemed the best way forward; on Shadsworth a Bootstraps initiative should be attempted; in South Bank (Langbaurgh) there were sufficient existing organisations to form the base of a One Stop Shop type initiative.

Secondly, there emerged in the early 1980s a renewed interest in community cooperatives and other forms of community business. Stimulated by the emergent interest in local economic initiatives at the end of the 1980s (Bramley, Stewart and Underwood, 1979) the community business movement drew heavily on a long tradition of cooperative enterprise stemming from Robert Owen (New Lanark) and the Rochdale Cooperative in the mid-nineteenth century (Pearce, 1993). The impetus given to cooperatives by the Highlands and Islands Development Board in the late 1970s, together with the widely recognised success of the innovative Craigmillar Festival Enterprises, created a climate in Scotland that stimulated community business over the following decade. By 1983 there were 20 community businesses in operation in Scotland (Hayton, 1983), and by the summer of 1985 their number had grown to over 60 (McArthur, 1986). Community business or community enterprise was not confined to Scotland (Centre for Employment Initiatives, 1986). Indeed, an early analysis of the potential and limitations of community business (Teague, 1987) argues from English inner city experience the fragility of community business initiatives. It highlights the very different types of such business that exist, the dangers of an over top-down approach, and the threat raised by over high expectations about the potential of community business. The evolution of Scottish experience remains the most significant for several reasons – the relative volume of community business experiments, the extent to which local government became involved in the support of community business and, lastly, the wealth of evaluation material (largely stemming from the University of Glasgow).

The significance of Urban Programme support in Scotland is central to the community business movement. Initially through Local Enterprise Advisory Project (LEAP) (Pearce, 1983), thereafter through Community Business Scotland and latterly through local authority support structures (notably Strathclyde Community Business Ltd) community-based enterprise received both financial support and managerial and financial advice. At the time, and in the light of the widespread failure of conventional employment structures, community business seemed to offer "potential for progressive experimentation" (McArthur, 1986).

Certainly the potential encouraged the DoE to commission an *Urban regeneration good practice guide* (DoE Inner Cities Directorate, 1990) based on 14 case studies, several on businesses based in estates. The 'community development base' section of the guide emphasises the importance of support agency outreach work, the necessity of financial support, and the need for development workers to ultimately let go. The guide also points to the need for "a community business actively to seek community support" (sic), to the need for collaboration and the avoidance of disputes or rivalries with others, and to the need to define the boundaries of individual and collective action. A similar (though more formally evaluated) good practice report (Cooper, Evans and Snaith, 1991) draws on action research in five housing estates (with four other estates receiving some coverage). The general aim of the action was explicitly to further the empowerment of local people, an aim pursued through six more specific objectives relating to support, research, feasibility studies, development work, pursuit of funding and evaluation of local interventions. The conclusions point to the need for both external influences (community attachment, organised networks, the policy environment) and internal influences (worker roles, organisational support) to be favourable; otherwise the effort is fruitless and counterproductive. 'Marked' out of a maximum 11 points two estates – Hattersley (Manchester) and South Docklands (Newham) – received nine positive rankings. The most significant element of this study seems to be the importance attached to community cohesion and the existence of some form of community base before conditions are conducive to economic initiatives.

By the early 1990s sufficient experience existed of community business to enable some longer term assessment to be made. Again, the Scottish experience is most significant (McArthur, 1993a, 1993b; McGregor, 1993) given that the Scottish community businesses were more advanced than others elsewhere. It is in the nature of neighbourhood-based business that the jobs available are concentrated around the estate and many relate to the maintenance of the housing stock, upkeep of the environment, protection of property and local services. Thus, painting, decoration, minor repairs, landscaping and maintenance of grounds, contract cleaning, security and launderettes are typical of the local jobs available. Many are low skilled jobs, part-time, and low paid. Thus the job profile in many ways reproduces the employment structure of the estate – unskilled, low paid and largely male jobs (70% of jobs in Scottish community businesses in 1990 were male jobs). There is conflicting evidence of the extent to which there is local recruitment. Some community businesses seem to recruit strongly from the local area (Gibson, 1993; Watson, 1994) and demonstrate high levels of targeting on local need. Others show far less local recruitment and move to the position where in order to win contracts and stay in business it is necessary to recruit labour more openly in the market (McArthur, 1993a).

Much community business is dependent upon contracts from supportive organisations, including local authorities, housing associations, cooperatives, and so on, with high levels of interdependence in the mid-1980s upon the Urban Programme and the Community Programme. The demise of the latter in 1988 brought severe problems to the community business movement.

The fragility of local linkages is reinforced by a number of examples where the membership of the community business (generally open to all residents) has fallen off with only the most strongly committed remaining active, as members of the business and/or as members of committees. It is common to find that these people are also active in other estate initiatives and/or in local council affairs, but this can create complications over possible conflict of interest in contracts. Other evidence suggests that older and well-established businesses hold their membership. The tension between commercial business goals and social community goals is a recurrent theme in community business studies. In many community businesses, therefore, there is some movement towards the involvement of members from outside the estate to the benefit of the business, if not necessarily to the community.

The strengths of community business are its potential to target upon local residents and to respond to local needs. Its weaknesses are the need for strong development support, the reliance (historically) on

IMPORTANT

public programmes such as the Community Programme (CP), the tension between commercial and social goals, the modest levels of local recruitment achieved in many cases, and the potential for rivalry with other local development agencies.

The contribution of community business to resident empowerment is, at best, ambiguous. There are notable successes where, as in Castlemilk, for example, local initiatives are supported by a local development agency (O'Toole, Snape and Stewart, 1995), but there are also numerous examples of community businesses that become disassociated with community interests and where the business quite reasonably becomes an end in itself. In addition to the most well-documented failures – Craigmillar (Hayton, 1982) and Barrowfield (McArthur, 1993a) – there is increasing evidence of the extent to which managerial failure, a hostile external economic environment, and the absence of sufficient or appropriate small business support combine to bring about community business failure.

Cooperatives involve local residents as shareholders rather than as members and provide a different form of accountability through shareholding (however small). The St John's project, Oldham (furniture repair and sale), Community Routes, Hyde (community transport but then diversified), Riverside Garden, Bristol (garden plants, sundries and advice), and the Gwynfi Cooperative, Blaengwynfi (mini market) are documented (DoE Inner Cities Directorate, 1990) as exemplifying good business practice (St Johns), successful diversification and commitment to social as well as financial audit (Community Routes), innovative funding and related legal structures (Riverside) and widespread community involvement in a local community project (Gwynfi). Cooperatives, with share ownership, are argued to offer more incentives to involvement than member-only community business, but the evaluation literature does not demonstrate whether this is true or not. In most other ways the cooperatives and other community business seem indistinguishable, with community commitment as well as advice and support from Cooperative Development Agencies (national or local) being crucial to start up and continuity.

The most recent 'movement' is that of Local Exchange Trading Systems (LETS). These systems represent the attempt to establish a non-money economy within the present general economic system by an extension of bartering. They allow people in the system to trade with each other using a form of 'local' currency (Bobbins, in

Manchester, Olivers in Bath, Favours in Bristol, Wharfes in Ilkley). A LETSystem is simply a directory of services that can be provided by members, and trading takes place without the need for any money (members credit each other using a local cheque book). There are some 140 LETSystems in Britain at present and perhaps 60 under development. The largest is the Manchester LETSystem (300 members); others are much smaller, originating with as few as 15 members. The nature of the work involved is local – cleaning, repair work, gardening, childminding – and essentially responds to community needs, depending upon a recognition of mutual needs and provision of services in the locality. The scope for LETSystems to operate at estate level as an alternative economic system for local services remains to be examined, but the essence of the initiative is essentially built around values of community and mutuality, concepts that figure strongly in community empowerment. As an alternative economic system offering the potential for exchange through a local monetary system the LETSystem remains in its infancy.

Most of the people on estates who are without formal work and wage rely on benefits. Welfare Rights campaigns, together with advice and information services, have held, and still hold great importance for the local economy insofar as increasing the level of benefits claimed not only helps individuals but also increases the circulation of money on the estate. Advice about access to benefits has become widespread both through community-based advice centres and through the money advice often offered by local authorities. New forms of poverty emerge, however, and there is increasing evidence of fuel poverty (reliance on expensive heating in inefficient buildings) and food poverty (reliance on expensive and unhealthy diet reinforced by the lack of access to health education and appropriate shopping facilities). A number of initiatives have begun to provide collective support to families in poverty through neighbourhood 'Healthy Eating' and 'Fuel Poverty' schemes.

Finally, credit unions represent a particular form and focus of collective action that supports individuals but also empowers by participation and representation. Responding to the high incidence of indebtedness on many estates, recognising the absence of fair and cheap credit, concerned about the impact of illegal or near legal lending practices and the absence of banks, credit unions (effectively, financial community cooperatives) provide the structure for local saving and lending. Credit unions numbered over 300 by the end of 1991 (McArthur, McGregor and Stewart, 1993), of which over 80%

were community credit unions. Estimates are that they involve over 50,000 people with assets approaching £20m. In terms of motivation for membership, savings patterns, borrowing, and place of residence, survey results (McArthur, McGregor and Stewart, 1993) suggest a more varied movement than is commonly appreciated. Dominated by the employed and self-employed, by people long resident in their areas (66% over 20 years resident), by women, and by people with one or more other accounts, credit unions fulfil a normal banking function for many middle and low income households. For those on lower earned incomes or the unemployed on benefits, access to the credit union is strongly associated with urgent need.

The creation of a credit union has been a basic goal of many community initiatives. In Hattersley (Cooper, Evans and Snaith, 1991) community action focused upon building a credit union and in three years membership had reached 375 people with assets of £30,000 – £22,000 had gone out in loans. The evaluation suggests that here the credit union was a success because it was a joint venture between tenants' association members, the community forum, and the community association, and 'new people' were involved. On a Plymouth estate (Watson, 1994) a credit union attracted 25 people in the first year with savings of £1,000. Nearly 200 children joined from a local primary school and saved £900 in six months.

Summary

All the above initiatives represent some form of collective management or provision, the wish to remain engaged in the local economy rather than exit. The first half of the 1990s has seen the run down of the Urban Programme and the emergence of City Challenge in England. Justified by an analysis that drew upon a major review of small area initiatives (Hausner, 1991) but was largely uninfluenced by the need to address polarisation and exclusion as well as fostering economic regeneration, the philosophy of large, public/private, integrated and coordinated comprehensive initiatives now holds sway. Such estate-wide initiatives are discussed further in a subsequent section of this report (pp 54-62).

The Urban Programme that provided support to a range of small-scale local projects is being wound down and the potential for bottom-up economic and employment initiatives may be being marginalised. Within these larger initiatives employment pro-grammes have a central place and some form of One Stop Shop or local economic development agency is generally found within them. Formalisation of local economic regeneration work within larger multi-sectoral initiatives may have blunted some of the specificity and local orientation that characterised many of the earlier estate-based community enterprise initiatives, and there is widely varying experience from the four Scottish Partnerships in terms of their employment impact.

The incorporation of community economic development into the mainstream of TEC and Employment Service oriented work could be beneficial. If such a mainstream offered better resourced support to community initiatives, and if main programmes were more clearly targeted, then the fragility of the community enterprise movement may be reduced. However, such incorporation could dilute the strength of the community input and lead to disillusionment and disempowerment.

Social consumption and quality of life

Social provision

Hausner, in his study of small area initiatives (1991) finds a striking lack of attention given to social and welfare schemes: "In almost every case where communities are asked for their views, the priorities are social: to do with crime prevention and the provision of amenities". He notes the absence of central government departments involved in health, welfare and education from formal partnerships, an absence that has persisted to the early months of the Single Regeneration Budget (Hill and Barlow, 1995). Hausner is critical, too, of the focus of most social initiatives on facilities and argues for more attention to be given to tackling crime and prostitution, to what he calls pre-economic activity and to tackling poverty and educational issues.

Other studies reinforce the view that housing and employment are not the only issues that are important to residents (Gibson, 1993; Cole and Smith, 1993; Ellis, 1988; Hastings, McArthur and McGregor, 1994 various; Barran, 1992). Crime, environmental issues, activities for children and young people are frequent concerns. Fear of crime, a deteriorating and bleak environment and lack of facilities all contribute to the poor image of the estate. Coupled with lack of resources and transport, these problems trap people in their own homes, reinforcing their personal sense of isolation and making it less likely that they will leave home to join in community activities. In addition, cuts in local authority expenditure have hit community facilities very hard.

Despite all this, social provision tends to be the poor relation in high profile initiatives to regenerate estates. Over the years the Urban Programme has placed less and less emphasis on social initiatives, and its replacement in England by the Single Regeneration Budget, with its emphasis on partnerships, is unlikely to signal a change of heart. In a number of the partnership projects studied by Hastings, McArthur and McGregor (1994 various) social issues have not been on the agenda and residents have had to fight to get them there. While Estate Action (now absorbed into the Single Regeneration Budget [SRB]) highlighted the need to tackle employment issues, it made no reference to social action, while the 1988 Housing Act makes no provision for housing associations to build community facilities (Page, 1994).

On the other hand, the integrated approach to estate regeneration now being adopted should allow not only for social issues to be more clearly articulated but can and does encourage innovative, community-based action.   The Scottish Partnerships illustrate the potential, with the Castlemilk Partnership offering important examples of community-based improvements in community care, education and health education and prevention advice.

There remains the tendency, most evident during the early years of community development, to see play provision and social welfare as 'soft' issues and housing, planning, income and employment as issues likely to provide political gains for the neighbourhood. This was a view much criticised by those concerned with gender and empowerment (Green and Chapman, 1992) and the invisibility of social issues does underline the invisibility of gender as an issue in estate empowerment, despite the fact that many of the leading activists are women (however, see Campbell, 1993).

Many of the accounts of estate regeneration underline the importance of social issues as the springboard of community action. It is in the social field that tenants often learn to organise and manage projects. Twenty-eight out of 40 of the small area schemes studied by Hausner (1991) tackled social and welfare issues and 12 were assessed as having social and welfare outcomes. Half the tenants' associations identified were engaged in community and social activities.

Early tenants' associations on estates were concerned with the effects of social isolation, as traditional family networks were broken up during slum clearance, and the lack of community facilities (Goetschius, 1969). On a stigmatised estate in North Wales with high unemployment, it was action on play that gave residents a sense of achievement and offered them the possibility of challenging the image of hopelessness given to them by outside agencies (Chanan, Hatch and Taylor, 1987). Community health surveys and activities (Roberts and Shepherd, 1990; Somerville, 1985) have been another route through which women in particular have been empowered and given a sense of control over their own bodies and their family's health.

Social action on Plas Madoc

The combination of a PEP-style decentralisation of housing management and the introduction of a community work team on this peripheral estate encouraged tenants to get involved in a wide range of activities. Vacant garages were cleaned out for community use, a local newssheet was established, playleadership training was set up and a multi-service centre established by the tenants' association (TA). This has housed welfare benefits advice, a women's group, a tool hire service, a darkroom – all run by the community – as well as services run by outside agencies. The TA also runs a Pensioners' Club and an umbrella group on the estate runs an Arts House with a varied programme for young people and adults. The Youth activity group on the estate runs youth clubs for different age groups, a video night, disco, an arts and crafts group, and holiday projects.

Central government policies in recent years have focused on the provision of choice: care packages in community care, and parental choice in education. The move to transfer community care and other services away from the public sector has also given community organisations the opportunity to deliver services on contract, although it remains to be seen how small local organisations will fare in the contracts market and whether they will be given sufficient resources to meet the considerable needs they have to address. Some community trusts, housing cooperatives and community-based housing organisations have moved into community care and education (Pearce, 1993; Hausner, 1991; McCall, 1987). Hausner cites the example of a 32-bed residential home set up by the Eldonians and a care scheme by New Routes in Hyde.

The lessons for estate regeneration and empowerment in this field, therefore, are not so much how to get residents involved or even how to give them control over their services. Some, in view of the lack of provision from outside, would say that social provision is already left too much in their hands. Sink estate policies in the past and community care policies now have housed vulnerable families and individuals in estates without the intensive back-up resources essential to their support (Lusk, 1988; Cole and Smith, 1993). Informal carers and hard-pressed community organisations have to substitute for diminishing statutory provision. Care in the community policies transfer vulnerable people to vulnerable areas. Meanwhile, residents continually see much-trumpeted estate regeneration initiatives spending money on projects that are not a priority for them and that sometimes cut across their own activities.

There is sense in which the issues raised by social needs are not specific to estates but apply across the board, even if the needs are more intense than in other areas. Donnison (1993) reminds us that not all deprived people live on estates and not all people in deprived areas are disadvantaged themselves. Two of the issues identified as priorities earlier in this section – crime and environmental improvement – do, however, have a particular relevance to estate regeneration.

Crime prevention

Hope and Shaw (1988) have argued that: "With only a little exaggeration, the problem estate has come to represent, rightly or not, the modern British image of the high crime community." This stereotype is exacerbated by the assumption that, on public housing estates, crime comes from within the community – an assumption that is not applied to other high crime areas (most Neighbourhood Watch schemes operate on the assumption that crime comes from outside and that the criminal is a stranger). In Scotswood, residents meeting with the police encountered the accusation that it was the community that was causing the problem (Lightfoot, 1994).

This assumption is often linked to a community pathology model (Whiskin, 1994), which sees crime on council estates as a failure of socialisation and community life. Page (1994) blames policies that have created an unbalanced population on the estate: "vandalism and incivilities are more likely when the ratio of children to adults is higher than normal, making it more difficult to exercise control". It is also possible to argue that, on estates where accepted routes to personal empowerment (such as a job) are unavailable, making money from criminal activity may be seen as a way of gaining respect among peers and may also be used as a form of social control.

All this means that estate residents have to face not only the disempowerment of the fact of crime, but also the disempowerment that goes with the stigmatisation of the whole area as being responsible for its high level of crime. Young people on estates are particularly vulnerable to stereotyping, despite the fact that they are usually the principal victims of crime (Gibson, 1993; Lightfoot, 1994).

Research suggests that fear of crime is as much the issue as how much crime there is (Safe Neighbourhoods Unit [SNU], 1993). Estates often experience a high level of what are nowadays called incivilities – littering, dog fouling, noisy parties, young people hanging about and behaving aggressively – which are not crimes but increase people's sense of insecurity and hence powerlessness.

> Old people are not just afraid to go out at night, they are afraid to stay in their homes during the day; before they collect their children from school, mothers hide their videos and tellies and radios, for fear they will be stolen while they are out; and there is menacing and deeply disturbing adult bullying and intimidation. (Whiskin, 1994)

Some environmental features common to disadvantaged estates evoke fear even when crime rates are low (walkways and long corridors are a prime example). But the SNU evaluation found that most council estates did not fall in the high risk band, although they were above average and council tenants were more likely to be burgled. The SNU study suggests that one explanation for the focus on estates in the demonology of crime is the fact that such estates are readily identifiable and that the fact that there is a single public landlord leads to the belief that crime on estates is resolvable. So, what has been done to turn around this pressure towards disempowerment?

Individual routes to individual empowerment tend to focus on the situational aspects of preventing crime. They include personal security measures and insurance, but many of these are not available to people on low incomes (Hope and Shaw, 1988). They also include environmental measures. In Waterfield, the local authority proposed putting a fence around an estate, ostensibly to prevent outsiders coming in, although local people suspected that the real reason was to protect a new build private estate close by (Lusk, 1988).

Part of the PEP programme has been explicitly concerned with using local management and coordination to combat crime. Features of its approach include beat policing, patrolling by caretakers, door security, reduced voids, and so on. In Cruddas Park there was a reduction of burglaries by 30% and reported crime went down by 25% through measures such as improved relations with the police, increased time on the beat, 24-hour caretaker schemes, and improved lighting in the shopping centre. But too much of a focus on security can dominate all other measures and reinforce labelling, while a massive police presence on one estate can simply move the problem elsewhere. And this approach risks a fortress mentality that can reinforce the sense of stigmatisation and the internalisation of a negative image for the estate. This is a particular problem if these are enforced in a vacuum, without the framework of community activity in a place like Cruddas Park or without the other aspects of the PEP programme.

A number of **collective** approaches to crime prevention have been identified: reducing the fear of crime (Morgan, 1991), preventing crime through security, environmental design, housing management and policing measures, and preventing criminal behaviour, through family, community and school-based activities (Bright, 1994).

The Safer Cities programmes have focused on a three-pronged approach:

- reducing crime

- reducing fear of crime

- encouraging a sound local economy as a means of generating a sense of well-being and safety.

This requires coordination between agencies and with the community. It is no good encouraging people to report crimes if all the telephone boxes on an estate are out of action because of vandalism. But, the Morgan report on 'Safer communities' comments that: "At present, crime prevention is a peripheral concern for all the agencies involved and a truly core activity for none of them" (Morgan, 1991).

The community, of course, is the exception. Crime prevention is central for people who live on the estate – and yet the community has rarely had much power in interdepartmental initiatives. There are a number of barriers to the effective involvement of communities in such initiatives. These include the contrast between agency and community perceptions; the diversity within communities them-selves; the frequent gaps between policy and implementation; and the failure to involve young people. Youth initiatives on Meadowell, for example, are piecemeal, involving a range of uncoordinated inputs. But youth crime initiatives there often fail to involve the community – a major and well-resourced multi-agency initiative was set up by the police with no community consultation, at a time when a lot of community effort was independently going into finding ways of revitalising the estate (Gibson, 1993).

Collective solutions to crime and fear of crime have to overcome the challenge of persuading people to leave their own homes and engage with others in airing fears and developing strategies. Women's self-defence classes and women's taxi firms are two obvious examples. In Scotswood and King's Cross, women have engaged in demonstrations to block streets and reclaim public space as communal territory, rather than the no-go areas that prostitution and crime turn them into. In Scotswood, a residents' newsletter reports progress on community anti-crime initiatives (Haq, Wall and Caffrey, 1994). Publicly speaking out against crime can be a risky business. On many estates (Broadwater Farm and Scotswood are two examples), a wider approach has included action on unemployment, childcare, domestic violence, and so on. Community enterprise has also had its contribution to make. There are several examples of community security firms in the literature (Pearce, 1993; Watson, 1994).

Youth and play provision are particularly important. Many community initiatives fail to involve the young people who are often the centre of concern over crime. Those working with young people around crime prevention initiatives emphasise the need to make connections between young people and the adult world and to make a serious investment in listening to what they have to say. But if it is difficult to involve the majority of adults in community initiatives, it is even more difficult to involve young people, who are unlikely to be interested in long-term, generalised programmes (Gibson, 1993). Nonetheless, work on Meadowell and elsewhere has shown that imaginative initiatives can engage young people. In Scotswood, for example, an initiative to encourage local residents to use local labour in their homes has helped to involve young people in their community (Haq, Wall and Caffrey, 1994)

In a number of areas, schools have been involved in estate redesign initiatives (Gibson, 1993; Watson, 1994). Schools have also introduced discussions on bullying, sexual harassment and other issues into the curriculum (Lightfoot, 1994). In a probation-run initiative called Project 33, young people who have outgrown the project go back to work with the younger children who have followed them, while Hausner cites a community project in St Paul's, Birmingham, which has set up a 30-place school for children with truancy records and behavioural problems.

Neighbourhood Watch schemes have been of limited value in estates – research suggests that they are less common here and only successful in more affluent areas. Bright (1993) warns of overdependence on community effort, alluding to experience in the US, where he believes too much is left to the community. This underlines yet again the fact that community control alone does not necessarily empower, if the community does not have the resources to deliver.

The lessons from social and crime initiatives on estates are similar. They involve lots of people and can engage different communities on the estate. They improve the image of the estate and demonstrate the capacity of residents. Indeed, the SNU report suggests that broad-based social and economic activities on estates make a major contribution to reducing crime. However, there is still a reluctance on the part of the authorities to consult enough, especially on crime issues. If the considerable resources that estate residents put into crime prevention and social regeneration initiatives are not to be wasted, the literature suggests that three things need to happen:

- Multi-agency estate regeneration initiatives that bring new resources to bear on estates need to take social concerns and activity seriously and to build upon the work already underway.

- The responsibility for responding to social and crime problems on estates should not be 'dumped' on individuals or community groups, but should be accompanied by sufficient resources and allow for community definition of priorities. This is especially important as social welfare services are 'privatised'.

- Resources for action in these areas must recognise the diversity of communities in estates that are often seen by outsiders as homogeneous. All sections of the community require access to the support they need and to have their particular concerns taken seriously rather than be scapegoated. Community-based facilities need to be accountable to the range of communities that need to benefit from them. Race and gender issues need to be addressed.

Design and the environment

Environmental improvements are central to initiatives to combat the fear of crime. Indeed, they encompass all of the issues discussed so far. Even though physical improvements alone are not enough, few initiatives can take place without considering the wider environment. And it is the environment that fashions the familiar image of the bleak estate, strewn with litter, broken glass and dog fouling, with broken down and abandoned facilities. The lack of differentiation between communal, public and private space means that there is no sense of ownership, and little care is taken of it. The SNU report quotes Wilson and Kelling's suggestion (1982) that: "Visible signs of neighbourhood deterioration are said by some to affect resident's perceptions of their areas, reduce informal controls and contribute to increases in crime" (Spray, 1992). American writers speak of the lack of 'defensible spaces' – areas over which people feel they have some control and which they can monitor (a concept promoted by Alice Coleman in this country). However, SNU argue that estate problems are still as much related to socio-economic and housing management factors and cuts in funding and resources as they are to design.

Nonetheless, a forbidding and uncared-for environment is likely to add to the sense of powerlessness that many residents feel, especially if it stops them from venturing out or having places for their children to play in sight. In the past, local authorities have exacerbated the problems by making changes without any community consultation: Gibson (1993) tells how gardens were turned into open space in Meadowell. Community facilities are built without consultation, which then lie unused or are beyond the means of local people (Chanan, Hatch and Taylor, 1987; Ellis, 1987).

One of the aims that Donnison and Middleton (1987) outline for urban regeneration projects in their account of Glasgow Eastern Area Renewal (GEAR) is to make declining areas 'nicer places' to live in, with physical improvements, management of pollution and public spaces adequately managed.   Several writers promote resident involvement in environmental improvements as essential to their sustainability: "A community that understands the reasons and values behind an environmental project will be more likely to respect and defend it and to help solve problems that arise in its use and maintenance" (Lusk, 1988). There are many examples in the literature of this principle being put into practice. MacFarlane (1993a) describes the refurbishment of an underused and vandalised park in Wolverhampton. It is not enough to landscape the environment – local communities need to be given the means and the motivation to maintain them.

It is difficult to envisage an individual form of environmental empowerment, although one of the advantages of Right to Buy and other measures to diversify tenure has been to tackle the depressing uniformity of council estates. But as a number of commentators have pointed out, the first sign of many estate initiatives has been the top-down redesign and rehabilitation project with little or no consultation with residents.

The PEP saw improvement of the environment as an important objective from the early 1980s when it was first set up. Power's 1984 evaluation finds four out of 20 projects involved in youth employment schemes to clean up estates, and four involved in reclaiming gardens from derelict land, with flowerbox competitions or children's planting projects, while seven had commissioned murals with the help of local children and schools. Nonetheless, Lusk's evaluation of various design projects suggests that participation in the design of the environment was still something of an innovation, and there are several examples of initiatives that have been blocked by authorities who considered that they 'knew better', who submitted bids for central government money and made no mention of tenant proposals or where tenants were sidelined in the face of interdepartmental conflicts over who should take the lead role (Lusk, 1988).

- A community-led design process can destabilise relationships within authority (Lusk, 1988). Technical officers resist local accountability and many departments are reluctant to accept formal responsibility of design professionals to the community. This was a problem in a Plymouth estate until the recruitment of a sympathetic architect and area housing manager (Watson, 1994).

- Environmental and design initiatives have an immense capacity for involving the community, as accounts of work on many estates show (eg, Watson, 1994; Gibson, 1993; Lusk, 1988; MacFarlane, 1993a; Newcastle Architecture Workshop, 1992). The use of 'Planning for Real' techniques (Gibson, 1988) and community arts projects across the country can not only attract people who are not interested in turning out for meetings, but can also involve children and young people.

- The execution of plans to improve the environment can then provide opportunities for jobs. In Meadowell, the community was involved in designing security grilles and the skills of redundant steel workers were used in their construction (Gibson, 1993). Design projects are fun and can be combined with social events: the caravan exhibition of plans in one area studied by Lusk acted as a temporary social centre, while Freeform, working in Goldsmith's Square had a celebratory festival when environmental projects were completed (Lusk, 1988).

- Planning needs to take account of resource constraints if plans are to be realistic and failure or disappointment avoided (Hastings and McArthur, 1995). However, a lot can be achieved, even in small-scale improvements, although the area studied by Lusk (1988) is critical of the piecemeal initiatives in Goldsmith's Square, where it feels the opportunity has been lost to give residents control over a comprehensive programme of improvements.

What are the lessons from this experience?

First, residents need to be involved at an early stage. Finished architects' drawings do not encourage participation – people need to be able to get hold of a pen and scribble on the design, and technical officers need to be involved from the start so that plans in which the community has an investment do not have to be torn up and the whole process started again. It is also a good idea to have a pilot scheme, so that the community can see, experience and take pride in its endeavours and so that their ideas can be tested in use.

Second, expert design advice under the residents' control is essential. Proposals can then be presented to the community and local authority in terms that are accessible, that make clear the constraints, but show empathy with consumers, link anxieties with solutions and demonstrate the contribution tenants have made in shaping the report. Lusk's (1988) evaluation, however, distinguishes between technical advice and community development support, suggesting that both are needed. Not every group of residents will want to do the design themselves. Lusk describes other projects where groups prefer to have a designer to prepare designs after consulting them, from which they can then choose. They need to be able to choose the degree of control they want.

Third, tenant involvement in design needs to be given time. There is a lot of criticism in the literature (Watson, 1994; Pinto, 1991; Pinto, 1993) of Estate Action timetables. On one estate, tenants put in two years hard work towards an Estate Action bid and the local authority invested money in expert support without any guarantee that the project would be supported (Watson, 1994). A proposal to add in support for the community arts work that was so crucial to the involvement of families across the estate almost ran out of time. As the 'icing on the cake', it was impossible to get it onto the tenants agenda before the Estate Action bid was approved and then there was a rush to build it into the contract specifications. Experience also suggests that it is essential that money is put into the budget for continued maintenance or else improvements will deteriorate and nothing will be gained.

Fourth, more commitment is needed to an equal partnership with residents. Estate Action contained no effective pressure on local authorities to cooperate with residents in the management and maintenance of schemes, even though resident involvement in management was a stated aim. Its financial timetables were a significant deterrent to such involvement.

Local authorities have resisted resident involvement in the past because they feel that residents do not understand the constraints. However, Watson suggests (1994) that residents are able to make compromises – in his study, residents traded a modicum of safety (ie, reinforced glass in upstairs windows) to find the money for some of the design work that they were proposing. The important point is that the compromises are their compromises.

Residents spend money differently from the way official agencies would do so and this can result in the more cost-effective investment of public money. It can also lead to a better cared for, better quality environment, with better use of community space and a more secure and caring environment, which can improve the image of the area. It has given residents on a number of estates the experience of working with professionals to a brief of their own making and in a way that has demonstrated to authorities what they can achieve.

There is still resistance to be overcome on the part of public authorities. There are issues, too, about whether this kind of activity simply creates flagship estates, with surrounding areas even more disadvantaged by comparison.

Hausner found that many of the physical regeneration schemes he studied were 'conventional' and he was surprised to find so little linkage to employment and business development. The experience to which we had access (eg, Hausner, 1991; McArthur, 1995; Gibson, 1993; Lusk, 1988; Watson, 1994) suggested that these links were being made in some cases. Indeed, the experience of one Plymouth estate involving residents in drawing up contracts that include a requirement for local training opportunities is now being adopted across the city (Watson, 1994). Both McGregor et al (1995) and MacFarlane (1993b) suggest that there may not be many local jobs in construction-related schemes – Watson (1994) found that few residents on his case-study estate took up the opportunities provided. However, the impact that providing even a few short-term opportunities can have on a demoralised community should not be underestimated.

Estate-wide partnership strategies

Earlier sections of this chapter have assessed progress on particular aspects of estate life: housing management, economic development, social consumption, safety and the environment. At each step, the authors have underlined the way in which different areas of activity on the estates overlap. Housing and environmental work can create opportunities for jobs; policies that encourage the transfer of community care and other services to independent organisations can also provide a boost to local enterprise (Cooper, Evans and Snaith, 1991). Pearce (1993) comments that the community enterprise activity he studied was as much focused on seeking viable ways of delivering local services as 'just jobs'. Housing management organisations move into social and economic activities (Pearce, 1993; DoE, 1989). Crime and environmental initiatives often involve a multi-service approach (SNU, 1993). As Hausner states:

> The place has to be improved in parallel with people's skills, job prospects and incomes. Tackling the latter without the former will result in people leaving the area as soon as they are able; tackling the former without the latter leads to physical deterioration after the place has been upgraded. (Hausner, 1991, p 11)

Many estates can boast a multitude of agency initiatives. Indeed, Gibson (1993) coins the term 'agency attack' to describe the invasion of outside agencies and interest into areas whose problems hit the media. But this section is concerned with estate-wide partnerships, where the intention is to build a coherent multi-agency, multi-service strategy.

Although partnership initiatives have mushroomed in recent years, the need to tackle estate regeneration as a multi-service, multi-activity endeavour has long been acknowledged. The seeds of estate-wide initiatives have been sown in such diverse places as the CDPs and Comprehensive Community Projects of the 1970s, in General Improvement Area legislation, and in the popular planning exercises of the GLC.

From the ground, some community workers sought to empower what were then called 'deprived areas' by building alliances between oppressed communities and other structurally oppressed groups in order to force change. Others adopted a more conciliatory social planning approach on the basis that "it is essential to maximise the human resources that can be made available to hard-pressed estates" (Henderson, Wright and Wyncoll, 1982).

From above, central government developed an increasingly targeted approach to urban regeneration, for example, with the increasing focus on designated partnership areas in the Urban Programme. It also moved towards partnership with the concerted attempt to give the private sector a lead in urban regeneration. More recently, City Challenge, the Urban Partnerships in Scotland and, most recently the Single Regeneration Budget, have pulled together a much wider range of policies in initiatives where, although employment has remained central, physical renewal, diversification of tenure, pubic participation, mixed use development and devolved decision making are also key features.

At the local level, estate-wide strategies have grown up in a number of ways: out of central government initiatives, from local initiatives to coordinate the activities of different levels of local government, and from housing work (deriving from community involvement or housing management professionalism).   Holmes (1992) concludes that local partnership initiatives tend to be tenant-led on the smaller estates and top-down on the larger estates. Some community-based housing associations and cooperatives have, however, grown into multi-purpose organisations – for example, in Liverpool (the Eldonians); Sparkbrook, Birmingham (SHAPE); Summerston, Glasgow. It is a process that has led Hausner (1991) to suggest that housing associations should be given the scope to broaden their remit beyond housing.

The community in partnership

A primary objective of top-down estate-wide initiatives has been to coordinate the efforts of the agencies involved on the estate, including those of the community. In some cases the vision goes beyond coordination to a concept of 'synergy', the added creativity that comes out of bringing different approaches and perspectives together (Mackintosh, 1993; MacFarlane, 1993a).

A number of different forms have been adopted for partnerships (MacFarlane, 1993a; Hastings and McArthur, 1995). Most have an overarching board with senior representatives from all partners and a series of issue-based and administrative subgroups, which involve a wider range of people. Some have a separate economic development arm or an intermediary structure to coordinate non-economic initiatives and/or community-based housing organisations. Community involvement is a standard feature of recent initiatives originating from government. Yet it is early days, and if the authors' concern in this report is with the extent to which communities are empowered by these mechanisms, then the conclusion from the literature thus far has to be sceptical, for a number of reasons.

- It is clear that community representatives are a minority on such boards and groupings. MacFarlane (1993a) reports that community representatives form an average of 25-30% of Community Challenge boards, with 20-30% of total expenditure subject to community consultation.   Two boards had no community representatives.   The amount of influence the community is allowed varies considerably.   The formality of meetings and the jargon used is generally alienating to community representatives and difficult to penetrate.   However, MacFarlane also cites some encouraging instances where community representatives have been involved in appointing senior staff (Deptford); where communities are involved in the allocation of funds (Wirral); and where there is a commitment to getting the support of the community's umbrella group for all spending decision (Middlesbrough).

- Their limited experience in formal mechanisms of this kind, added to the disparity between their own resources and those at the disposal of other agents, places community representatives at a considerable disadvantage in respect of time and resources, particularly at the beginning of an initiative. As already seen from the experience of Action on Estates, requirements from central government to involve the community take little account of the resources and time required to build up a successful and credible partnership with the community. The short lead-in time to the initial City Challenge meant that community involvement was low (MacFarlane, 1993b) and the New Life Urban Partnerships in Scotland either failed to involve the community in their design or seriously underestimated the time required to allow for an effective input (Hastings, McArthur and McGregor, 1994 various). Groups without resources are particularly disadvantaged: "What we are talking about is partnership between two first division teams and another struggling to get into the Vauxhall GM league" (Wallace, 1992).

There is a dominance of inter-agency agendas with much of the energy of partnership initiatives focused on setting up workable mechanisms for relationships between agencies. The committees are geared more to the needs of the lead agencies than to the community. Thus, PEP evaluations report that: "The ambitious nature of some partnership schemes resulted in far more energy going into sorting out internal LA arrangements than into involving residents and other agencies" and add that "Collaborative action often reflects agency agendas rather than plans derived for the estate."

The success of coordinating mechanisms depends on leadership and commitment. Despite the rhetoric, many of these initiatives are 'bolt-on' (Hastings and McArthur, 1995; Bright, 1994) and have little impact on mainstream activity or on the culture of agencies such as local government as a whole. Even in those areas where residents are best equipped to participate, agencies and departments involved in partnerships continue to act as if the initiative wasn't happening (Bright, 1994; Hastings and McArthur, 1995).

In the King's Cross Community Benefit Area, community participants became increasingly frustrated over the first 18 months that nothing was happening. The Area subcommittees added to the bureaucracy rather than establishing a fast track. It was only when the leader of the council and the chief executive called a meeting with chairs and chief officers in the authority to underline the priority status of this committee that progress began to be made.

Even where bottom-up initiatives have been successful, outside agencies continue to operate as if they do not exist. Thus, Gibson (1993) reports a major crime prevention project that was put into Meadowell by the police without consultation and a large neighbourhood office that was built for the local authority at a time when community plans were being stalled. This is demoralising and demonstrates yet again to the community the imbalance in power between them and their 'partners'. On the other hand, larger initiatives with longer time-scales can have lasting impacts on the attitudes and behaviour of local government officials. In Castlemilk, evaluation identifies explicit shifts in the practices of education and health offices after the initial years of partnership (O'Toole, Snape and Stewart, 1995).

Hastings and McArthur (1995) found that partnership committees were often rubberstamping mechanisms with the real work going on either in subcommittees, to which community organisations have variable access, or in informal behind-the-scenes activities, to which communities have no access. Community representatives can easily find themselves sucked into the demands of time-consuming formal mechanisms and away from their constituencies. Indeed, partnership agendas, as determined by lead agencies, often come to dominate community agendas. Community representatives have few sanctions. MacFarlane (1993a) suggests that "pulling the plug" is not necessarily an effective sanction and that "the hassle potential" is a far more effective community weapon.

Partnership structures tend to act as overseeing and ratifying bodies rather than forums for debate.   Jacobs sees them as "organisational working arrangements with a private sector input" (Jacobs, 1995, p 40), which tend to increase rather than decrease bureaucracy. Accounts of partnership (Hastings and McArthur, 1995; Jacobs, 1995) illustrate how consensus drives out debate and how few communities are able to stand out against this consensus model. It seems that the Lukes analysis of power is highly significant in these initiatives. Community issues seldom seemed to get onto the agenda and communities declare themselves satisfied with achievements that in no way match up to the rhetoric of partnership.

The literature suggests that genuine community involvement is most likely where community structures and initiatives have developed over a long period of time and with support from community development or other specialist workers. Hastings, McArthur and McGregor (1994 various) suggest that even experienced community organisations can be destabilised by their involvement in multi-agency partnerships. Experience from many other studies suggests that, if community involvement has no tangible results, community structures are undermined and overworked and the credibility of local representatives and leaders suffers. The introduction of high-profile competitive bidding for resources only ups the stakes and increases the risk of disappointment (Jacobs, 1995). Community involvement is thus a high risk strategy for communities themselves.

In the housing field, tenants' organisations have questioned the value of getting sucked into formal mechanisms and have taken the decision to campaign from outside the system (Taylor, Sheffield and Newcastle Tenants' Federation, 1986). In many estates where partnership initiatives have not been set up, but where communities are active, more informal mechanisms exist for coordination with outside bodies. This may give them greater control. Although they miss out on the additional resources and high profile provided by partnership initiatives like the City Challenge or the Scottish Urban Partnerships, they may be able to resist incorporation or even takeover.

As an alternative to the partnerships discussed above, community trusts are "independent, not for profit organisations which take action to renew an area physically, socially and in spirit" (Warburton and Wilcox, 1988). Community Development Trusts (CDTs) are multi-sector and are widely committed to community involvement. However, the legal nature of a trust and the way in which it operates does not in itself guarantee a strong community presence and the extent to which residents play an important role varies widely. Arguably, none of the nine trusts described by Warburton and Wilcox are estate-based, though several undertake activities that impinge upon estates and their residents and seek to improve the image and conditions of the area – but for many trusts empowerment of residents is not per se a primary driving force.   Fitzpatrick and Jackson (1992) suggest that less than a quarter of an estimated 100 development trusts have a community representation majority on their management committees or boards.

Representing the community

Holmes (1992), in her study of peripheral estates, stresses the difficulties of developing structures to coordinate community activity and to bring community views together.   Most estates in the City Challenge areas studied by MacFarlane had forums to channel views into the decision-making process as did the initiatives studied by Hastings, McArthur and McGregor (1993 various).   Typically, community organisations or neighbourhood forums feed into one or two central assemblies or umbrella bodies, which then nominate or elect the two or three community representatives on the board, although community representatives may also be involved in subcommittees.   In some cases separate forums are established to ensure that minority ethnic groups are adequately represented.

MacFarlane (1993a) comments that often the decision on the representative structure was made by the authority. This was less often the case in the Scottish Urban Partnerships, but evaluation research shows how the demands of Partnership either created new umbrellas within their areas or contributed to changes in existing structures, usually to improve their geographical coverage and to bring in elections (Kintrea et al, 1995; Gaster, 1995; O'Toole, Snape and Stewart, 1995; McGregor, 1995).

The success of umbrellas depends on community traditions and how far estate residents identify with the whole estate or with smaller neighbourhoods within the estate.   Participation in an umbrella organisation requires a degree of energy and commitment that a number of groups on the estate will not have. For many people it is easier to relate to a tangible local service or campaign than to a more abstract idea of a participation in an umbrella or partnership.   In Meadowell, for example, despite the considerable energy and imagination that went into Planning for Real in relation to the Village, some local activities remain at arm's length (Gibson, 1993). A clear separation has also been made between the executive role of the trust and the need for a body to represent community views. A separate forum, which is represented on the trust, allows people from the estate to meet separately to discuss issues and to formulate views.

Two problems constantly recur with community representative structures. One is that, if open, they are still vulnerable to being dominated by professionals; the other, that their legitimacy may be questioned by other partners (who, as MacFarlane points out, rarely subject their own credentials to the same scrutiny). There is a need for partnership bodies to be much clearer about what can be expected of representatives. Hastings, McArthur and McGregor (1994d) and O'Toole, Snape and Stewart (1995) suggest that particular problems are presented in the case of community representation on economic development agencies, where people who are elected as representatives are expected to act as company directors.

There is a need for those involved in estate-wide initiatives to unpack what is expected from representation and what is a realistic expectation.

Summary

Area-based initiatives have changed in the last five years from the relatively numerous but still small-scale interventions based on housing management and providing increased voice for tenants, into a phenomenon that is both larger in scale and in the number of agencies involved. The Single Regeneration Budget and the Scottish Urban Partnerships are the extreme examples of this shift.

Empowerment through or in partnership has the potential to be quite different from empowerment through consultation, parti- cipation, or involvement in service programmes (notably housing). In theory it provides the community with the right to a seat at the table on an equal basis with other partners, which in turn requires other partners to negotiate rather than pulling rank, to develop alliances and coalitions, to mediate conflict through consensus building and compromise. These new 'rules of engagement' cast a fresh light on old questions – about the relative strength of the several partners, the procedures and agendas of partnership, the location of formal and informal decision making, the availability of information and the way in which it is communicated. Traditional power relations between central government, local authority and community are being mediated in a new organisational setting.

The effectiveness of these new circuits of power remains unproven. The earliest evaluations of the Scottish Urban Partnerships are qualified in their endorsement of the community dimension (William Roe Associates, 1994; McArthur, Hastings and McGregor, 1994), though all studies acknowledge the depth of involvement and participation. The evidence suggests that, although more than lip service is being paid to community interests, there is a long way to go before residents on estates are in any sense in control of the resources going into their communities and the strategies that are being formed to regenerate them. Reviewing MacFarlane, West (1994) argues that, while it may be an unpalatable truth: "The community must learn to behave in the same way as those with greater power". The power-holders define the agenda – a clear demonstration of Lukes' second face of power.

It is now the conventional wisdom that Partnership is the way forward. It is also to be the way forward for urban policy in England and Wales, with the Single Regeneration Budget. Cooper, Evans and Snaith (1991) warn, however, against programmes adopting wide-ranging objectives that are addressed towards alleviating problems caused by long-standing forms of social deprivation. Gibson (1993) believes that: "mega schemes are long in preparation and once launched, they wallow on like overloaded oil tankers. It takes an age to cope with the unexpected and change course". He underlines the value of small schemes as opposed to mega schemes from outside. Other writers add their weight to this point of view (Whiskin, 1994; Lusk, 1988; Spray, 1992), while Hausner (1991) stresses how "tackling too much leads to managerial problems and lack of effectiveness". In the light of this weight of opinion, the decision to abandon the Urban Programme looks as potentially dangerous today as it did when it was first announced.

5

CONCLUSIONS

It seems that little has been learned from past experience. Although the ideological, political and professional context for community participation changes over time, the same issues about lack of power and about the limited access for community interests to power structures appear and reappear in the literature. There is little evidence of systematic evaluation, there is extensive reinvention of wheels, government initiatives towards communities and estates seem to draw less on experience and more on expedience. All these indications of a lack of learning have implications for longer term capacity building on estates and for the sustainability of estate-based community initiatives.

The failure of 40 years of participation and involvement to shift established power structures suggests that the starting point for final reflections should be the lack of power and of disempowerment. Harman argued that the "world economy in its present form has as one of its main products marginal people – the unemployed, the underemployed, the disenfranchised – people who lack [...] a sense of belonging and of having a recognised role" (1993, p 1069). One community studied in the literature was described not as a community but rather as a

> ... selection of people living very isolated lives, unrelated to each other. These are people with very low confidence, a very low level of skill and perceived nil access to jobs and training .... In practice, when you are living on benefit just below the poverty line, what choices can you make about your life? (Cole and Smith, 1993)

Holmes (1992) echoes this view, arguing that empowerment initiatives on estates need to start by first removing the most obvious barriers to empowerment – financial worries and unemployment, as well as poor housing conditions. Evaluations of Urban Partnership for The Scottish Office highlight the deep-seated conviction of the local community that poverty lies at the heart of their problems (Gaster et al, 1995; O'Toole, Snape and Stewart, 1995; Corden and Mackenzie, 1995).

Cole and Smith (1993) stress how far estates are disempowered as much by stereotyping as by the reality:

> The stereotypical image of the estate has made it difficult, even with a lot of consultation, to distinguish between the real and imaginary problems that [the estate] faces.

Taylor, Kestenbaum and Symons (1976) charted the negative effects of stereotyping, whereby residents internalise and accept the negative image of the estate, which is then reinforced by the behaviour of outside agencies who refuse credit, leave it to rot, and treat it as a sink estate, with the result that only people who appear to fit the label will go there. To reverse this spiral requires that residents are given the confidence to shatter the stereotype, and that outsiders begin to treat the estate differently. The danger is that attempts to regenerate the estate will continue to be undermined by stereotypes that bear little relation to current reality.

Redefining empowerment

Four levels of disempowerment can be identified:

* **Isolation** – reinforced through the personal internalisation of 'failure' and by negative images and stereotypes from outside.

* **Dependency** – on services and income planned, provided and managed by others, who themselves may be demoralised and controlled by distant bureaucracies.

* **Marginalisation** within schemes to regenerate or rehabilitate the area. Power flows around and over the community not through it.

* **Exclusion** – from the basic rights and access to income, housing, employment, and services, an exclusion that is often enshrined in political inaction and administrative practice.

Because exclusion is both at the beginning and end of the process (isolation derives from poverty and lack of access to the services and labour markets), this can be represented as a cycle of disempowerment.

Empowerment requires that this cycle is reversed, as illustrated in Figures 3 and 4 (see p 66).

Countering isolation through individual empowerment, building local capacity and realising existing strengths

Cole and Smith (1993) argue that, given the high levels of unemployment on the estate they studied, "the degree of stability on the estate, the positive views of most residents and the low level of recorded crime all appear as quite remarkable, rather than exceptionally problematic". Despite the poor image of many estates and the disempowerment of residents, many studies demonstrate the inherent strengths of local communities and the strong attachment that residents have to them (Baldwin, 1993; Holmes, 1992; Cole and Smith, 1993; Donnison, 1993; Thake and Staubach, 1993). The sink estate stereotypes conceal the stability, warmth, enthusiasm, skills and energies, which, in practice, exist within local communities, even if realisation of these strengths is difficult and even if confidence has drained from individuals and communities.

The first step in empowerment, therefore, is to build the confidence of the people who live on the estate, to realise the assets that already exist there but which are undervalued, and to energise the networks (and potential circuits of power) that are latent within the estate. One route is through individual empowerment, through giving people rights to choice through the market (eg, Right to Buy), or access to a job, or better security and providing the support and advice to help them make individual choices. Localised services and clearly defined standards can also give people more sense of being in control – the evidence certainly suggests that this is the case. Individual empowerment can, however, be considerably enhanced by collective community action and approaches that give people a sense of the assets they have in their community already. There are hundreds of examples of small-scale community development activities that show people what assets they already have in their estate (skills surveys are one example), that build on the capacities of local people or groups and offer modest local empowerment through shared activity.

Figure 3:   A cycle of disempowerment

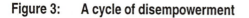

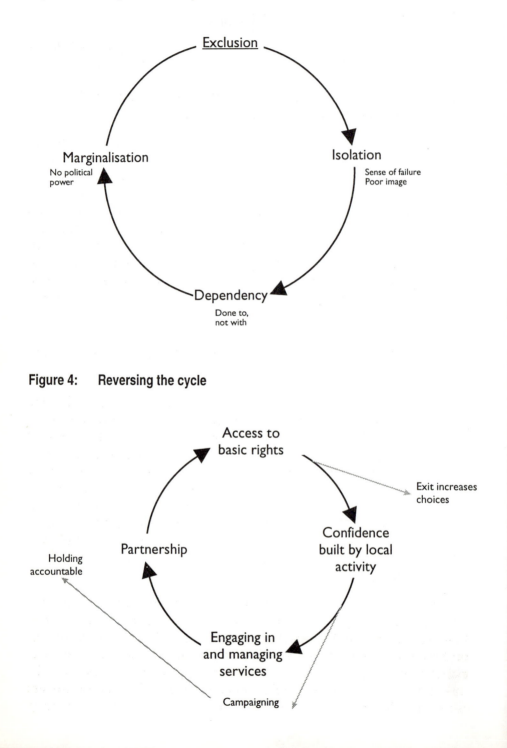

Figure 4:   Reversing the cycle

The negative side of this empowerment is its fragmentation, its small-scale, limited impact, its potentially competitive nature (as one initiative fights another), the absence of learning beyond the immediate experience, the exploitation (and burn out) of committed people (largely women), who give their all to sustain and support community life in the face of considerable odds. Indeed, for some, such modest local empowerment simply diverts attention from the more exploitative structures of power in society.

The strengths and potential of such empowerment, however, are the recognition of local assets, the ability to start from small beginnings, the potential for involvement and ownership, and the fact that relatively limited resources can release considerable energies. Estates are peppered with community initiatives that have come from the bottom up and which, if allowed to grow and develop, provide a modest but important degree of local empowerment. Such empowerment is a positive-sum game – there need be no real loss of power by others, and the power gained by communities is valuable but not threatening to stronger and more entrenched power structures.

Reducing dependency by empowering service users and changing the nature of service delivery

Empowerment on estates is seen by some (and certainly by the government) as releasing local communities from the burden of state bureaucracy and giving them much more say over the nature of local service delivery. Dominated by the shifts in housing (see chapter 4) this form of empowerment may involve simply more voice over services, new consumer rights, or charters and other routes to complaint and appeal. It may also involve more direct managerial or ownership roles, or the substitution of alternative collective forms of provision. There are signs that initiatives to give people control over jobs and services seem to have progressed further in Scotland than in the rest of the UK.

The strengths of this form of empowerment are evident in a number of service areas and offer more resident control over services. However, there are dangers if estate residents take on responsibilities without appropriate resources. Offering control without the means to exercise that control does not constitute empowerment. Nor do the interminable delays and complex procedures that characterise current resource allocation processes even for small amounts of money.

Offering such control should also not be allowed to detract from residents' capacity for campaigning and representative activity on a wider scale. Local control of services is not always either desirable or possible.

Approaches at this level need to recognise that not everyone wants to be involved in running services. The evidence suggests that people have cycles of involvement. People may be willing to get involved at some point in their life and not at others or in some kinds of activities (eg, estate design) and not in others. People need to choose how they will be empowered and how they will have access to different degrees of control. There are many guides to participation and how to involve people at different levels, and their lessons need to be absorbed.

More control also needs to be supported by resources. The move from campaigning to running services requires new skills, responsibilities, accountabilities and an adjustment to new roles and demands. New power relationships within the community can de-stabilise existing networks and even cause resentment. Giving estate residents control also requires that existing power holders (eg, local and health authorities) move into an enabling instead of a providing role. There is an essential role for government in supporting these developments, but it is a different role from that of the monopoly service provider.

Preventing marginalisation through radically new structures of area governance

Formal regeneration policy has moved on from the twin track of Housing Improvement (and latterly Action on Estates) on the one hand and Urban Programme support on the other, into a phase of integrated, multi-organisational, coordinated, and large initiatives taking an estate-wide view. First City Challenge and now the Single Regeneration Budget (SRB) (where they operate on estates) as well as Urban Partnerships in Scotland reflect this approach.

The 'community' is, in principle, one of the key stakeholders in the new estate regeneration strategies. Local people are expected to be involved (albeit at an extraordinary speed) in the design of bids or strategic plans. There is community representation at 'the top table' on partnership boards, committees, forums, and so on. Community accountability is presented as a crucial element of monitoring and evaluation.   There is therefore potential for a considerable shift of power in the new structures of area governance as communities are invited to become players in a bigger game with significant resources, with the programmes of central and local government apparently under scrutiny, and with access to information about the estate.

Here again, however, the potential for empowerment is offset by danger.

- Sometimes what is given with one hand to flagship projects is taken away with another from mainstream budgets.

- Participation in partnerships is hard work for inexperienced people from communities.

- Representation on a major partnership committee is fraught with difficulties and vulnerable to manipulation.

- The skills of bargaining, negotiation, and coalition building are more complex than those of complaining or demanding.

- The motivations and power games of civil servants, local authorities, quangos and the private sector are (probably) unfamiliar to community participants.

- The distinction between real and symbolic policy is difficult to fathom.

For all these reasons, the new politics and structures of estate-wide or area governance offer both significant empowerment to local communities and also the threat of marginalisation in an even larger arena than hitherto.   They also increase the risk of exposing and exacerbating divisions within the community, insofar as partnership demands consensus.

The difficulties of squeezing the diversity of community into a unified structure have already been emphasised.   Rather than pressing community 'umbrella' bodies towards an unattainable goal of representation, suggested by the idea of a unified community, it is necessary to unpick what is being asked of representatives and to ensure both that they have the resources and information to reflect the range of local needs and priorities as effectively as possible, and that the opportunities are there for local people to hold them appropriately accountable.   The issue is not just one of mechanisms and structures or even of resources.   It is possible that too much emphasis is put by agencies and community structures alike on presenting a unified view. The recognition of conflicting interests may be the first step to real empowerment. Rather than allowing conflict to divide and rule, however, solutions need to be found to local problems that are able both to meet the needs of different communities on an estate and to define and act on overarching common interests. Otherwise, partnership and the consensus it requires will become just another way of disempowering those who do not conform.

Fighting exclusion by shifting underlying structures of society

The fundamental right to income and access to basic material goods and services (housing, benefits, job opportunities, health, and so on) are not likely to be debated and delivered within local community politics. When residents seek to place such issues on the agenda of partnership they often meet resistance. Insofar as estate residents are empowered through such a route, it is because national political agendas place 'local' issues in the sphere of open politics. The poll tax and sale of council houses were two such issues. Others have included the right to repair, the introduction of CCT, new structures for community care, and local management of schools. In practice, the material conditions of life on estates will be determined by the outcome of political struggle over such issues at national and international level. The extent to which local communities can be empowered by action in relation to such questions begs the whole question of the nature of political action and the relationship between grass roots politics, social movements, political mobilisation, and local, national and international struggle.

In this sense, the debate about empowerment goes wider than the Joseph Rowntree Foundation Action on Estates Programme aspires, although structures that empower communities at the estate or area level and that build knowledge of and confidence about the broader processes of resource allocation may become the springboard from which this final level of community empowerment takes off.

Moving through the cycle

To move through the cycle of empowerment described, it is necessary to bring into the open the discussion about power, its location and use that was begun in chapter 3. The further we move around our cycle, the more closed and difficult the nature of policy formulation and decision making becomes. The small-scale gains that are achieved and are possible at the local level, which build upon local resources and aspire to modest change in personal and community life, do not raise major issues for the political agenda. Power is not threatened. Nor do changes in service delivery threaten the major structures of power greatly, although they do undermine the position of those who have long held control over the local allocation and delivery of resources. Moving round the cycle of empowerment, however, the issue of what gets onto the agenda and what is concealed becomes more significant. Informal power structures resolve issues before public debate is resolved; accountabilities that are raised as a major issue for residents are not even questioned elsewhere in the system. Much is still taken for granted. At the highest level, certain issues are screened out completely, either formally through political debate and decision, or less obviously through the unconscious assumptions that are central to the analysis of the third face of power.

For the community, this means that issues and possibilities go off the agenda without even being acknowledged, and labels and restrictions are accepted without even the recognition that they are being imposed from outside. For power-holders, it means that cultures are in place, which at every step obstruct the sharing of power. For much of the time, power-holders are not even aware of the ways in which they hold onto power – they do not recognise the impenetrability of their language and procedures or the extent to which these have to be changed; they do not recognise the extent to which they frustrate the community's ownership even of their own structures as they insist on access and dominate meetings to which they are invited.

The danger is that new forms of partnership or corporate governance will incorporate residents into existing circuits of power or marginalise them as mere spectators of the realignment of power among the existing institutions of governance. If power is to be transformed, it is not only power-holders who need to recognise the need to embark on the painful process of change. New networks of power need to be developed and alliances forged that open up new circuits and render old ones redundant.

Finally, in relation to power, attention needs to be paid to the way in which different forms of exclusion interact. Gender and race are not issues that appear often in the literature studied outside the specialist feminist or equalities literature. As this report only too clearly reflects, they are given little more than a footnote in the literature on estates, despite the fact that it is women who are usually at the forefront of estate action, or that minority ethnic groups are themselves scapegoated within estates. Yet the politics of identity offers both insights and warning signals to our understanding of power within estates, as the earlier historical account suggests. If empowerment is not to turn into further fragmentation, the issues it raises have to be confronted. In this sense, as Bea Campbell (1993) shows graphically in her analysis of the 'yob culture', estates act out in microcosm the challenges that face the wider society. The interaction between spatial and other forms of exclusion requires much more attention than it has received hitherto.

Summary

This final chapter has described the cycles of disempowerment and empowerment that the literature on estates has described over the years. It has also demonstrated that the various strategies for empowerment that have been tried over the years are not mutually exclusive. Each step expands people's choices as to how to move on, but each step also depends on the one before. Comments have been made in earlier sections on the dangers of eclipsing small-scale activities with 'high status' large-scale initiatives. The ability of estate residents to engage with the mega-initiatives and of communities to hold their representatives accountable depends crucially on the capacity and confidence built through the small-scale initiatives that open up the cycle of empowerment. The diversity of involvement that these initiatives allow ensured that the diversity of communities on any estate can feed into wider political processes. Diversity also allows for innovation and resilience. The pursuit of the mega-initiative and of a consensus approach can swamp the foundations of local activity and suck community leaders out of their constituency and into a process that is not of their making. The point needs to be underlined again that the resources formally channelled through the Urban Programme and other government initiatives to develop local voluntary action are essential to empowerment.

Finally, *sustainability* is essential to empowerment. Sustainability is a term more familiar in the realm of environmental politics, but it is highly relevant to estate regeneration and the question of "how to encourage stable and self-generating environments" (Evans, 1994). It is a metaphor with considerable potential in this field. Top-down initiatives need to build an exit and succession strategy into their thinking from the start, and the impetus, energy, commitment and resources that are brought by the large-scale partnership initiative need to be tied to a long-term view, that goes well beyond the life of political administrations. This, above all, is the reason for building real power in estates – as has been said in the body of the report, the professionals and the agencies can come and go. It is the residents who will go on living there and whose children will be born there.

REFERENCES

[This literature review covered material published up to the end of 1994, although some material has been added from 1995.]

Arnstein, S. (1969) 'A ladder of participation in the USA', *Journal of the American Institute of Planners*, July.

Bachrach, P. and Baratz, M.S. (1962) 'Two faces of power', *American Political Science Review*, 56.

Baldwin, J. (1993) 'Urban criminality and the "problem" estate', *Local Government Studies*, October.

Barran, S. (1992) *Partnership at work: creating cooperative working relations between housing staff and tenants*, London: Priority Estates Project Ltd.

Boaden, N., Goldsmith, M., Hampton, W. and Stringer, P. (1982) *Public participation in local services*, London: Longman.

Bootstrap Enterprises, Hackney, and MacFarlane, R. (1989) *Economic development on housing estates*, London: Priority Estates Project Ltd.

Bramley, G., Stewart, M. and Underwood, J. (1979) 'Local employment initiatives', *Town Planning Review*, xx, vol 50.2.

Bright, J. (1994) 'The multi-agency approach', in J. Lightfoot (ed), *Towards safer communities: community development approaches to crime*, London: Community Development Foundation in association with Crime Concern, pp 20-22.

Bright, J. (1993) 'Youth crime prevention and social policy', in R. Hambleton and M. Taylor, *People in cities*, Bristol: SAUS Publications, pp 131-54.

Burns, D., Hambleton, R. and Hoggett, P. (1994) *The politics of decentralisation*, London: Macmillan.

Cairncross, L., Clapham, D. and Goodlad, R. (1992) 'The origins and activities of tenants' associations in Britain', *Urban Studies*, vol 29, no 5, pp 709-25.

Campbell, B. (1993) *Goliath: Britain's dangerous places*, London: Methuen.

Chartered Institute of Housing/Tenants' Participatory Advisory Service (1989) *Tenant participation in housing management*, London: CIH/TPAS.

Chanan, G., Hatch, S. and Taylor, M. (1987) *After the pay-off*, London: Community Projects Foundation and Clywd County Council.

Clapham, D. and Kintrea, K. (1992) *Housing cooperatives in Britain: achievements and prospects*, London: Longman.

Clegg, S. (1989) *Frameworks of power*, London: Sage.

Cohen, S. (1985) *Visions of social control*, Cambridge: Polity Press.

Cole, I., and Smith, Y. (1993) *Bell Farm in the midst of change*, Centre for Regional Economic and Social Research, Sheffield Hallam University.

Cooper, L., Evans, M., and Snaith, R. (1991) *Owning our own: community enterprise in housing estates*, London: Community Economy Ltd.

Corden, A. and Mackenzie, M. (with C. Norris) (1994) *Living in Castlemilk*, Edinburgh: Central Research Unit, The Scottish Office.

Craig, G. (ed) (1980) *Community work case studies*, London: Association of Community Workers, 2nd edn.

Craig, G. (1989) 'Community work and the state', *Community Development Journal*, 24.1, pp 3-18.

Croft, S. and Beresford, P. (1992) 'The politics of participation', *Critical Social Policy*, 12.2, pp 20-43.

Dale, J. and Derricourt, N. (1990) 'Dilemmas in housing-oriented community development', *Community Development Journal*, 25.1, pp 66-74.

Daniel, W.W. (1972) 'Whatever happened to the workers at Woolwich?' Political and Economic Planning, Broadsheet 507.

Dearlove, J. (1974) 'The control of change and the regulation of community action', in D. Jones and M. Mayo, *Community work one*, London: Routledge and Kegan Paul.

Department of the Environment (1989) *Tenants in the lead – the housing cooperatives review*, London: HMSO.

Department of the Environment Inner Cities Directorate (1990) *Community businesses: case studies of good practice in urban regeneration*, Report prepared by Land and Urban Analysis, London: HMSO.

Dickson, J. and Robertson, I. (1993) *Taking charge*, London Housing Unit.

Donnison, D. (1993) 'The challenge of urban regeneration for community development', *Community Development Journal*, 28.4, pp 293-98.

Donnison, D. and Middleton, A. (1987) *Regenerating the inner city: Glasgow's experience*, London: Routledge and Kegan Paul.

Du Guy, P. and Salaman, G. (1992) 'The cult(ure) of the customer', *Journal of Management Studies*, 29.

Duncan, P. (1989) *Cooperative housing*, London: Institute of Housing.

Ellis, S. (1988) 'Not just a housing problem', special issue on 'Peripheral estates', *Housing and Planning Review*, Dec/Jan 1987/88, pp 20-21.

Evans, R. (1994) 'Planning, sustainability and the chimera of community', *Town and Country Planning*, April, pp 106-8.

Foucault, M. (1980) *Power/knowledge: selected interviews and other writings*, C. Gordon (ed), Brighton: Harvester Press Ltd.

Frankenberg, R. (1966) *Communities in Britain: social life in town and country*, Harmondsworth: Penguin.

Gaster, L. (1995) *Ferguslie Park Partnership: an evaluation*, Edinburgh: Central Research Unit, The Scottish Office.

Gaster, L. and Taylor, M. (1993) *Learning from the consumer and the citizen*, Luton: Local Government Management Board.

Gibson, T. (1988) *Making it happen: a user's guide to the neighbourhood action packs*, Telford: Neighbourhood Initiatives Foundation.

Gibson, T. (1993) *Danger: opportunity: a report to the Joseph Rowntree Foundation on Meadowell Community Development for the Neighbourhood Initiatives Foundation*, Telford: Neighbourhood Initiatives Foundation.

Glennerster, H. and Turner, T. (1993) *Estate based housing management: an evaluation*, London: HMSO.

Goetschius, G.W. (1969) *Working with community groups: using community development as a method of social work*, London: Routledge; New York: Humanities Press.

Green, J. and Chapman, A. (1992) 'The British Community Development Project: lessons for today', *Community Development Journal*, 27.3, pp 242-58.

Gregory, S. and White, J. (1991) *Front line housing management: a summary of progress on 21 PEP Partnership Projects*, London: Priority Estates Project Ltd.

Gyford, J. (1976) *Local politics in Britain*, London: Croom Helm.

Hambleton, R. and Taylor, M. (1993) *People in cities*, Bristol: SAUS Publications.

Haq, J., Wall, M. and Caffrey, J. (1994) 'Stop crime against residents', in J. Lightfoot (ed), *Towards safer communities: community development approaches to crime*, London: Community Development Foundation in association with Crime Concern, pp 24-25, 36-37.

Harman, W.W. (1993) 'Rethinking the central institutions of modern society: science and business', *Futures*, December, pp 1063-70.

Hastings, A. and McArthur, A. (1995) 'A comparative assessment of government approaches to partnership with the local community', in R. Hambleton and H. Thomas (eds), *Urban policy evaluation*, London: Paul Chapman Publishing, pp 175-93.

Hastings, A., McArthur, A. and McGregor, A. (1994a) *Community participation and partnership in estate regeneration project: case study report no 1: the Drumchapel initiative*, University of Glasgow: Training and Employment Research Unit.

Hastings, A., McArthur, A. and McGregor, A. (1994b) *Community participation and partnership in estate regeneration project: case study report no 2: the Wester Hailes Partnership*, University of Glasgow: Training and Employment Research Unit.

Hastings, A., McArthur, A. and McGregor, A. (1994c) *Community participation and partnership in estate regeneration project: case study report no 3: the Greater Easterhouse initiative*, University of Glasgow: Training and Employment Research Unit.

Hastings, A., McArthur, A. and McGregor, A. (1994d) *Community participation and partnership in estate regeneration project: case study report no 4: the Castlemilk Partnership*, University of Glasgow: Training and Employment Research Unit.

Hastings, A., McArthur, A. and McGregor, A. (1994e) *Community participation and partnership in estate regeneration project: case study report no 5: Meadow Well Development Trust*, University of Glasgow: Training and Employment Research Unit.

Hausner, V. and Associates (1991) *Small area-based urban initiatives: a review of recent experience, vol 1: main report*, London: V. Hausner and Associates.

Hayton, K. (1982) 'Why did Craigmillar crash?', *Initiatives*, November.

Hayton, K. (1983) 'Employment creation in deprived areas: the local authority role in promoting community business', *Local Government Studies*, Nov/Dec.

Hayton, K. (1990) *Getting people into jobs: case studies of good practice in urban regeneration*, prepared for DoE, London: HMSO.

Henderson, P. (1983) 'The contribution of CDP to the development of community work', in D. Thomas (ed), *Community work in the eighties*, London: National Institute for Social Work.

Henderson, P., Wright, A. and Wyncoll, K (eds) (1982) *Successes and struggles on council estates: tenant action and community work*, London: Association of Community Workers in the UK.

Hill, S. and Barlow, J. (1995) 'Single regeneration budget: hope for "those inner cities"', *Housing Review*, 44.2, pp 32-35.

Hirschman, A. (1970) *Exit, voice and loyalty: responses to decline in firms, organisations and states*, Harvard: Harvard University Press.

Hoggett, P. and Hambleton, R. (eds) (1987) *Decentralisation and democracy: localising public services*, Occasional Paper 28, Bristol: SAUS Publications.

Holmes, A. (1992) *Limbering up: community empowerment on peripheral estates*, Middlesbrough: Radical Improvements for Peripheral Estates.

Hope, T. and Shaw, M. (1988) *Communities and crime reduction*, London: HMSO.

Jacobs, K. (1995) 'Partnership: some home truths', *Housing Studies*, 44.2, pp 40-41.

Joseph Rowntree Foundation (1995) *Inquiry on income and wealth*, York: Joseph Rowntree Foundation.

Khan, U. (1989) 'Neighbourhood forums: the Islington experience', *Local Government Policy Making*, 16.2.

Kintrea, K., McGregor, A., McConnachie, M. and Urquhart, A. (1995) *Interim evaluation of the Whitfield Partnership*, Environment Research Programme Research Findings No 11, Edinburgh: The Scottish Office Central Research Unit.

Lightfoot, J. (ed) (1994) *Towards safer communities: community development approaches to crime*, London: Community Development Foundation in association with Crime Concern.

Lowery, D., de Hoog, R. and Lyons, W.E. (1992) 'Citizenship in the empowered locality', *Urban Affairs Quarterly*, 28:1, pp 69-103.

Lukes, S. (1974) *Power: a radical view*, London: Macmillan.

Lusk, P. (1988) *Working together for a better environment: how the community technical aid movement is supporting residents of housing estates*, Wolverhampton: Partners in Charge.

MacFarlane, R. (1993a) *Community involvement in City Challenge: a good practice guide*, London: National Council for Voluntary Organisations.

MacFarlane, R. (1993b) *Community involvement in City Challenge: a policy report*, London: National Council for Voluntary Organisations.

MacFarlane, R. and Mabbott, J. (1993) *City Challenge: involving local communities*, Moss Side and Hulme Community Development Trust and National Council for Voluntary Organisations.

Mackintosh, M. (1993) 'Partnership: issues of policy and negotiation', *Local Economy*, 7.3.

McArthur, A. (1986) 'An unconventional approach to economic development', *Town Planning Review*, 57.1.

McArthur, A. (1993a) 'An exploration of community business failure', *Policy and Politics*, 21.3.

McArthur, A. (1993b) 'Community business and urban regeneration', *Urban Studies*, 30.4/5, pp 849-73.

McArthur, A. (1993c) 'Community partnership – a formula for neighbourhood regeneration in the 1990s?', *Community Development Journal*, 28.4, pp 305-15.

McArthur, A. (1995) 'The active involvement of local residents in strategic community partnerships', *Policy and Politics*, 23.1.

McArthur, A., Hastings, A. and McGregor, A. (1994) *An evaluation of community involvement in the Whitfield Partnership*, Edinburgh: Central Research Unit, The Scottish Office.

McArthur, A., McGregor, A. and Stewart, R. (1993) 'Credit unions and low-income communities', *Urban Studies*, vol 30, no 2, pp 399-416.

McCall, F. (1987) 'Back to the future in housing', special issue on 'Peripheral estates', *Housing and Planning Review*, Dec/Jan 1987/88.

McGregor, A. (1993) 'Housing expenditure and neighbourhood economic development', *Local Economy*, 7.4.

McGregor, A., Fitzpatrick, I., McConnachie, M. and Thom, G. (1995) *Building futures: can local employment be created from housing expenditure?*, Joseph Rowntree Foundation Housing and the Construction Industry Research Programme, Bristol: SAUS Publications.

McGregor, A., Kintrea, K., Fitzpatrick, I. and Urquhart, A. (1995) *Interim evaluation of the Wester Hailes Partnership*, Environment Research Programme Research Findings No 14, Edinburgh: The Scottish Office Central Research Unit.

McRafferty, P., Riley, D. and the Department of the Environment (1989) *A study of cooperative housing*, London: HMSO.

Meegan, R. (1989) 'Paradise postponed: the growth and decline of Merseyside's outer estates', in P. Cooke (ed) *Localities*, London: Unwin Hyman.

Maslow, A.H. (1954) *Motivation and personality*, New York: Harper and Row, 2nd edn (1970).

Meekosha, H. (1993) 'The bodies politic – equality, difference and community practice', in H. Butcher, A. Glen, P. Henderson and J. Smith, *Community and public policy*, London: Pluto Press.

Morgan, J. (1991) *Safer communities: the local delivery of crime prevention through the partnership approach*, Report for the Home Office Standing Conference on Crime Prevention.

Morris, P. (1993) 'Citizens and health care', in R. Hambleton and M. Taylor (1992) *People in cities*, Bristol: SAUS Publications, pp 214-34.

Newcastle Architecture Workshop (1992) *1977-1992: a celebration of fifteen years of achievement*, Newcastle: Newcastle Architecture Workshop.

O'Toole, M., Snape, D. and Stewart, M. (1995) *The Castlemilk Partnership: an evaluation*, Edinburgh: Central Research Unit, The Scottish Office.

Page, D. (1994) *Developing communities*, Sutton Hastoe Housing Association.

Pearce, J. (1983) 'Leap into business', *Initiatives*, August, p 38.

Pearce, J. (1993) *At the heart of the community economy: community enterprise in a changing world*, London: Calouste Gulbenkian Foundation.

Penn, R. (1987) 'Stockbridge Village Trust', special issue on 'Peripheral estates', *Housing and Planning Review*, Dec/Jan 1987/88.

Pinto, R.R. (1991) 'Central/local interaction in renovating run-down estates – the view of housing authorities on the Estate Action Initiative', *Local Government Studies*, 17.1, pp 45-62.

Pinto, R.R. (1993) 'An analysis of the impact of Estate Action schemes', *Local Government Studies*, 19.1, pp 37-55.

Power, A. (1984) *Local housing management*, London: Department of the Environment.

Power, A. (1987) *Guidelines for setting up new projects* (The PEP Guide to Local Housing Management, 3), Department of the Environment, Welsh Office, Priority Estates Project Ltd.

Power, A. (1988a) *Small scale employment creation on unpopular estates*, London: Priority Estates Project Ltd.

Power, A. (1988b) *Under new management*, London: Priority Estates Project Ltd.

Power, A. (1991) *Running to stand still*, London: Priority Estates Project Ltd.

Power, A. (1992) *Empowering residents*, paper to OECD Project Group on Housing, Social Integration and Livable Environments in Cities, Paris: Organisation for Economic Cooperation and Development.

Power, A. (1994) *Area-based poverty, social problems and resident empowerment*, Discussion Paper WSP/107, STICERD, London School of Economics and Political Science.

Richardson, A. (1979) 'Thinking about participation', *Policy and Politics*, 7.3, pp 227-44.

Roberts, E. and Shepherd, M. (1990) *'We live there, we should know': a report on local health needs in Hartcliffe*, Bristol: Hartcliffe Health Project.

Safe Neighbourhoods Unit (1993) *Crime prevention on council estates*, London: HMSO.

Seabrook, J. (1984) *The idea of neighbourhood: what local politics should be about*, London: Pluto Press.

Seebohm, Lord (1968) *Report of the committee on local authority and allied personal social services*, Cmnd. 3703, London: HMSO.

Seligman, M.E.P. (1975) *Helplessness*, San Francisco: WH Freeman.

Servian, R. (1993) *Perceptions of power*, MSc dissertation, Bristol: SAUS, University of Bristol (forthcoming as publication by The Policy Press).

Sinfield, A. (1970) *What unemployment means*, Oxford: Martin Robertson.

Skeffington, Lord (1969) *People and planning: report of the committee on public participation in planning*, London: HMSO.

Smith, J. (1993) *Community development and tenant action*, London: Community Development Foundation and National Coalition for Neighbourhoods.

Somerville, G. (1985) *Community development and health*, London: London Community Health Resource.

Spray, W. (1992) *Taking the reins: a case-study of the Hornsey Lane Estate Management Board*, London: Priority Estates Project Ltd.

Tajfel, H. (1981) *Human groups and social categories: studies in social psychology*, Cambridge: Cambridge University Press.

Taylor, M. (1995) 'Community work and the state: the changing context of UK practice', in G. Craig and M. Mayo (eds), *Community empowerment: a reader in participation and development*, London: Zed Press.

Taylor, M. and Presley, F. (1987) *Community work in the UK 1982-86: a review and digest of abstracts*, London: Library Association Publishing and Community Development Foundation.

Taylor, M., Kestenbaum, A. and Symons, B. (1976) *Principles and practice of community work in a British town*, London: Community Development Foundation.

Taylor, M., Newcastle and Sheffield Tenants' Federation (1986) 'For whose benefit? Decentralising housing services in two cities', *Community Development Journal*, 21.2, pp 126-32.

Taylor, M., Means, R., Hoyes, L. and Lart, R. (1992) *User empowerment in community care: unravelling the issues*, DQM11, Bristol: SAUS Publications.

Teague, P. (1987) 'The potential and limitations of community business in local economic development', *Local Government Studies*, July/Aug.

Thake, S. and Staubach, R. (1993) *Investing in people: rescuing communities from the margin*, York: Joseph Rowntree Foundation.

Thomas, D. (1983) *The making of community work*, London: George Allen and Unwin.

Turok, I. and Wannop, U. (1990) *Targeting urban employment initiatives*, University of Strathclyde for DoE, HMSO.

Twelvetrees, A.(1983) 'Whither community work', in D. Thomas (ed), *Community work in the eighties*, London: National Institute for Social Work.

Wallace (1992) in N. Bailey and A. Basker, *City challenge and local regeneration partnerships: conference proceedings*, London: Polytechnic of Central London.

Warburton, D. and Wilcox, D. (1988) *Creating development trusts: case studies of good practice in urban regeneration*, prepared for DoE, London: HMSO.

Watson, D. (1994) *Tenants in partnership – driving force for renewal of the Pembroke Street Estate, Plymouth*, York: Joseph Rowntree Foundation.

West, A., (1994) 'Pushing in the debate: review of community involvement in City Challenge', *SEARCH* 19, pp 21-22.

Whiskin, N. (1994) 'The experience of Crime Concern', in J. Lightfoot (ed) *Towards safer communities: community development approaches to crime*, London: Community Development Foundation in association with Crime Concern, pp 7-8.

William Roe Associates (1994) *An evaluation of community involvement in the Ferguslie Park Partnership*, Edinburgh: Central Research Unit, The Scottish Office.

Wilson, J. and Kelling, F. (1982) 'Broken windows – the police and neighbourhood safety', *The Atlantic Monthly*, March.

Zipfel, T. (1989) *Estate management boards: an introduction*, London: Priority Estates Project Ltd.

FURTHER BIBLIOGRAPHY

(1988) 'User-controlled community technical aid: a symposium', *Town Planning Review*, 59 (1).

Armstrong, J. (1993) 'Making community involvement in urban regeneration happen – lessons from the United Kingdom, *Community Development Journal*, 28.4, pp 355-61.

Ash, J. (1982) 'Tenant participation, Part 1: a review of techniques', *Housing Review*, March-April, 31.2, pp 54-55.

Bailey, N. and Barker, A. *City Challenge and local regeneration partnerships: conference proceedings*, London: Polytechnic of Central London.

Baldwin, J. (1975) 'Urban criminality and the "problem" estate', *Local Government Studies*, 1.4, pp 12-20.

Banks of the Wear Community Housing Association, Bell Farm Residents' Association, York City Council, Newcastle Architecture Workshop Ltd, Joseph Rowntree Foundation (1992) *Planning our future: the action plan*, Newcastle: Newcastle Architecture Workshop.

Batley, R. (1975) 'An explanation of non participation in planning', *Policy and Politics*, vol 1, no 2.

Benington, J. (1974) 'Strategies for change at the local level: some reflections', in D. Jones and M. Mayor (eds), *Community work: One*, London: Routledge and Kegan Paul.

Bernstock, P. (1991) 'The dirty end of the trickle-down process', *Town and Country Planning*, 60:11/12, pp 331-32.

Birchall, J. (1988) *Building communities the cooperative way*, London: Routledge and Kegan Paul.

Birchall, J. (1994) *Notes on research into tenant participation*, prepared for the Third Ruskin Seminar on Community Development, Oxford, February.

Blewitt, H. and Garratt, C. (eds) (1993) *Tenant participation in housing associations: report of two workshops*, London: Community Development Foundation in association with Tenant Participation Advisory Service Midlands and The Housing Corporation.

Bright, J. (1986) 'Creating an effective voice', *Housing*, April.

Brown, G. (1988) 'On tap not on top', *Housing*, June/July.

Bruton, M.J. (1980) 'Public participation, local planning and conflicts of interest', *Policy and Politics*, vol 8, no 4, pp 423-42.

Burbridge, M. (1992) *More than bricks and mortar: resident management of American public housing*, London: Department of the Environment.

Burton, P. and Stewart, M. *Family stress and community action: an evaluation for Cheshire County Council of areas of family stress policies and community action area initiatives*, University of Bristol: School for Advanced Urban Studies.

Butcher, H., et al (1993) *Community and public policy*, London and Colorado: Pluto Press.

Centre for Employment Initiatives (1986) *Communities in business*, Liverpool: Community Initiatives Research Trust.

CES Ltd (1984) *Outer estates in Britain: a 'framework for action'*, Part 1: a *discussion paper* (CES Paper 28).

Chamberlayne, P. (1978) 'The politics of participation: an enquiry into four London boroughs, 1968-74', *The London Journal*, 4.1.

Clapham, D. and Kintrea, K. 'Importing housing policy: housing cooperatives in Britain and Scandinavia', *Housing Studies*, vol 2, no 3, pp 157-69.

Clapham, D. and Kintrea, K. (1987) 'Public housing', in D. Donnison and A. Middleton (eds), *Regenerating the inner city: Glasgow's experience*, London: Routledge and Kegan Paul.

Clapham, D., Kemp, P. and Kintrea, K. (1987) 'Cooperative ownership of former council housing', *Policy and Politics*, vol 15, no 4, pp 207-20.

Clarke, M. and Dalton (1979) 'Walking the planning plank: community planning initiatives in Lothian', *Corporate Planning Journal*, 6.2.

Clarke, M. and Stewart, J. (1992) *Citizens and local democracy: empowerment: a theme for the 1990s*, Luton: Local Government Management Board.

Commission of the European Communities, Directorate General XVI-Regional Policies (1993) *Quartiers en crise: citizenship laboratories for Europe?*, Final Report, Programme 1991-93, EC.

Community Projects Foundation (1988) *Evaluating community initiatives: report of the conference held on 12 October 1988 in Glasgow*, London: Community Projects Foundation.

Croft, S. and Beresford, P. (1990) *From paternalism to participation: involving people in social services*, Open Services Project/Joseph Rowntree Foundation.

Cruddas Park Community Trust Ltd (1991) *Annual Report*, Newcastle-upon-Tyne.

Cupps, D.S. (1977) 'Emerging problems of citizen participation', *Public Administration Review*, 38/5, pp 478-85.

Dawes, T. (1990) 'Reclaim, rebuild and revive', *Employment Gazette*, December.

Dawson, J. (1991) 'Housing cooperatives: from housing improvement to economic regeneration?', *Local Economy*, May.

Department of the Environment (1984) *Local housing management: a priority estates project survey*, consultant A. Power, London: Department of the Environment.

Department of the Environment (1993) *Crime prevention on council estates*, prepared by the SNU for the DoE, London: HMSO.

Department of the Environment (1993) *Working together to make life better: report of conference proceedings*, Estate Action Conference held at Ditton Community Centre, Widnes, 6 July.

Diamond, J. and Nelson, A. (1993) 'Community work: post-local socialism', *Community Development Journal*, vol 28, no 1, pp 38-44.

Dickson, J. and Robertson, I. (1993) *Taking charge*, London: Housing Unit.

Duncan, T. (1994) 'Community councils and the reform of local government in Scotland', *Local Government Policy Making*, 20.4, pp 45-52.

Estate Action Update (1992/93) Issue 1.

Firn Crichton Reports Ltd et al (1986) *Employment opportunities for Wester Hailes: final report*.

Flynn, N. (1989) 'The "new right" and social policy', *Policy and Politics*, vol 17, no 2.

Gallant, V. (1992) 'Community involvement: North Tyneside's approach', *Local Government Policy Making*, vol 18, no 4.

Gibson, T. (1979) *People power: community and work groups in action*, Harmondsworth: Penguin.

Gibson, T. (1986) *Us plus them? A starter kit to remake the neighbourhood – for residents, prospective residents and local authorities*, London: Town and Country Planning Association.

Gibson, T. (1991) 'Out of the ashes...', *Town and Country Planning*, October.

Goodchild, B. (1987) 'Local authority flats: a study in area management and design', *Town Planning Review*, 58 (3).

Goodlad, R. (1985) *Tenant participation: onward and upward?* (forthcoming)

Hall, N. (1993) *From participation in initiatives ... to initiatives in participation: developing a people-centred approach*, Manchester: The Urban Regeneration Consultancy.

Hambleton, R. and Hoggett, P. (1993) 'Rethinking consumerism in public services', *Consumer Policy Review*, 3, 2.

Hand, S. (1992) 'Getting its hands dirty', *Employment Gazette*, November.

Holmes, C. (1988) *Tenant involvement on PEP estates*, London: Priority Estates Project Ltd.

Institute of Housing and Royal Institute of British Architects (1988) *Tenant participation in housing design: a guide for action*, London: Institute of Housing and Royal Institute of British Architects.

James, S., Hosler, S.J. and Allmarsh, T. (1983) 'Evaluating a community action scheme', *Community Development Journal*, 18.1, pp 20-32.

Johnson, W.C. (1984) 'Citizen participation in local planning: a comparison of US and British experiences', Environment and Planning C: *Government and Policy*, vol 2, pp 1-14.

Kettleborough, H. (1989) 'Involving the community in equal opportunities initiatives: International Women's Day events', *Local Government Policy Making*, vol 16, no 3, 37-41.

Loney, M. (1983) *Community against government: the British Community Development Project 1968-78 – a study of government incompetence*, London: Heinemann Educational Books.

Malpass, P. (1979) 'Two faces of community action', *Policy and Politics*, vol 7, no 2, pp 181-96.

Mars, T. (1987) 'Mersey Tunnel vision?', *Roof*, Nov-Dec.

McKie, R. (1974) 'Cellular renewal: a policy for the older housing areas', *Town Planning Review*, 45 (3).

McGregor, A., McArthur, A. and Noone, V. (1988) *An evaluation of community business in Scotland*, Edinburgh: The Scottish Office.

Means, R. and Smith, R. (1988) 'Implementing a pluralistic approach to evaluation in health education', *Policy and Politics*, vol 16, no 1.

Miller, C. and Bryant, R. (eds) 'Community work in the UK: reflections on the 1980s', *Community Development Journal*, 25.4.

Morton, R.R. (1973) 'Housing renewal at Port Sunlight', *Town Planning Review*, 44/4.

Morton, T. (1991) *Dogs on the lead: good practice for dogs on housing estates*, London: Priority Estates Project Ltd.

Mottram, L. (1991) 'Reclaiming the role of the community – CTAC at Chell Heath', *Town and Country Planning*, January, pp 14-15.

Ogilvey, G. (1986) 'Making the periphery the centre of attraction', *Initiatives*, June.

O'Toole, M. (1992) 'Participation in the community: problems and possibilities', *Going Local*, 19, pp 8-9.

Parson, D. (1987) 'Housing and autonomy: theoretical perspectives on non-statist movements', *Housing Studies*, 2.3, pp 170-76.

Platt, S., Piepe, R., and Smyth, J. (1987) *Heard or ignored: tenant involvement in housing associations*, National Federation of Housing Associations.

Power, A. (1987) *The PEP experience* (The PEP Guide to Local Housing Management, 2), Department of the Environment, Welsh Office, The Priority Estates Project Ltd.

Power, A. (1987) *The PEP model* (The PEP Guide to Local Housing Management, 1), Department of the Environment, Welsh Office, The Priority Estates Project Ltd.

Priority Estates Project Ltd (1982) *Improving problem council estates: a summary of aims and progress*, consultant A. Power, London: Department of the Environment.

Richardson, A. (1977) *Getting tenants involved: a handbook on systems for tenant participation in housing management*, London: Department of the Environment.

Richardson, A. (1977) *Tenant participation in council housing management*, London: Department of the Environment.

Roberts, J. (1988) 'New brooms for old problems', *Employment Gazette*, pp 365-70.

Robinson, F. and Shaw, K. (1991) 'Urban regeneration and community involvement', *Local Economy*, 6.1.

Robinson, K., Shaw, K. and Lawrence, M. (1993) 'More than bricks and mortar?', *Town and Country Planning*, June.

Rosener, J.B. (1978) 'Citizen participation: can we measure its effectiveness?', *Public Administration Review*, pp 457-63.

Rubin, H.J. (1993) 'Understanding the ethos of community-based development: ethnographic description for public administrators', *Public Administration Review*, Sept/Oct.

Satsangi, M. and Clapham, D. (1990) *Management performance in housing cooperatives: a report to the Department of the Environment*, London: Department of the Environment.

Shaw, P. (1991) 'Estate of the art', *Housing*, Dec/Jan.

Smith, G. and Cantley, C. (1984) 'Pluralistic evaluation', in J. Lishman (ed), *Research highlights*, Aberdeen: Department of Social Work.

Smith, J. (1984) *Public participation in local government*, London: Community Development Foundation.

Spray, W. (1992) *Taking the reins*, London: Priority Estates Project Ltd.

Stewart, M. and Taylor, M. (1993) *Community leadership*, Luton: Local Government Management Board.

Taylor, M. (ed) (1988) *Releasing enterprise: voluntary organisations and the inner city*, National Council for Voluntary Organisations.

Tenant Participation Advisory Service (Wales) *Making a start: a report on tenant participation in Wales*, Cardiff: Tenant Participation Advisory Service.

Tenant Participation Working Group (1988) *Working to help each other: report for consultation*, Tenant Participation Working Group.

Thompson, J. (1991) 'The spirit of the place', *Town and Country Planning*, pp 36-37.

Tudor, C. (1990) 'The employment service and inner cities', *Employment Gazette*, August.

Westington, N. and Phillips, S. (1985) *Explanatory note on the agreement between the Cloverhall Tenant Management Cooperative and the council*, London: Priority Estates Project Ltd, Working Paper 2, Department of the Environment: Urban Housing Renewal Unit.

Wilcox, D. (1992) *The guide to effective participation*, Brighton: Partnership Books.

Wilcox, D. (1994) *An A to Z of partnerships*, Brighton: Delta Press.

Wilcox, S., et al (1993) *Local housing companies: new opportunities for council housing*, York: Joseph Rowntree Foundation.

Willmott, P. and Hutchinson, R. (eds) (1992) *Urban trends 1*, London: Policy Studies Institute.

Wimpey, G., PLC (1993) *Making it happen through partnership: a review of housing issues and initiatives*, London: G. Wimpey.